Yale Linguistic Series

An Introduction to the Burmese Writing System

by D. Haigh Roop

New Haven and London, Yale University Press

1972

Printed in the United States of America by
The Murray Printing Co., Forge Village, Massachusetts.

Distributed in Great Britain, Europe, and Africa by
Yale University Press, Ltd., London; in Canada by
McGill-Queen's University Press, Montreal; in Latin
America by Kaiman & Polon, Inc., New York City;
in Australasia by Australia and New Zealand Book Co.,
Pty., Ltd., Artarmon, New South Wales; in India
by UBS Publishers' Distributors Pvt., Ltd., Delhi;
in Japan by John Weatherhill, Inc., Tokyo.

CONTENTS

PREFACE

This book has developed from my experiences in learning the Burmese and
Thai writing systems. In 1961, when I first began the study of Burmese, I
found learning to read and write a lengthy and tortuous process. Three years
later I was introduced to the Thai writing system by way of Edward M. Anthony's
A Programmed Course in Reading Thai Syllables (Ann Arbor, 1962). Although
both languages are written with an Indian alphabet, the Thai system is mark-
edly more complex than that of Burmese; yet through Professor Anthony's
excellent presentation I was able to learn Thai writing far more quickly and
easily than I had Burmese. This experience has lead me to apply the programmed approach to Burmese writing in the hope that such a book may ease the
study of Burmese for future students as Professor Anthony's did my study of
Thai.

To those familiar with the Burmese writing system, some aspects of the
arrangement of this book may seem arbitrary. For example, in Chapter 1 why
are the consonants and vowels not presented in alphabetical order? It is
believed that the benefits to be gained from such an ordering are outweighed
by the pedagogical advantages of the approach used here, which derives from
limitations imposed by the presentation of the vowels. In order to introduce
the "constellation" form of the written syllable as early as possible, the
book begins with a small set of consonants on which to build syllables, after
which one vowel symbol is presented in each of the four positions occupied by
such diacritics around the initial consonant. To facilitate the student's
assimilation of these syllable structures, those vowels are presented first
which avoid the problems of tonal representation -- that is, the four level
tone symbols. Since in the Cornyn transcription such syllables are unmarked
for tone, there is no need to mention this difficult subject at first, and
the student is left free to concentrate on the basic written syllable form.

One consequence of this approach is that, contrary to normal practice,
/loun:ji: tin hsan hka'/ and /hnahcaun: ngin/ are presented before their
tone III counterparts. A second is that the velars cannot be introduced as
the first set of consonants on which to build syllables, since they do not

occur with /loun:ji: tin hsan hka'/. A presentation in alphabetical order is
thus precluded, but phonetic order is preserved in the introduction of the
consonants by progressing from the labials to the velars.

In the other chapters the ordering is either alphabetical or based on
grouping together elements which follow similar patterns in the writing struc-
ture.

Many people have provided help and advice during the preparation of the
text. Special gratitude is due Mr. John Okell of the School of Oriental and
African Studies, University of London, whose extensive comments on an earlier
description of the writing system form the basis for part of the organization
of this book, particularly Chapters 3 and 4. Professor F. K. Lehman of the
University of Illinois has commented most helpfully on two versions of the
manuscript. Both The Burmese Writing System, by Robert B. Jones, Jr., and U
Khin (ACLS, Washington, 1953), and an outline of the writing system prepared
by Mrs. Anna Allott for students at the University of London have provided
valuable checks on my information. In addition, both Professor Jones and U
Khin have given helpful advice on the text. Also of great help in making
revisions and improvements were comments and suggestions from several of my
students who worked through an earlier version.

Special thanks are also due Daw Tin Tin both for her help with writing
the large demonstration characters and for her patience in checking and
proofreading the Burmese parts of the text.

New Haven, Connecticut   D. Haigh Roop
June 1971

INTRODUCTION

1. History.

The extent of early Indian cultural influence on continental Southeast
Asia is nowhere more apparent than in the use of Indian writing systems for
non-cognate languages covering large parts of the latter area. While these
writing systems are all derived from the devanāgarī alphabet of Sanskrit, the
spread of writing from one people to another can, in part, be traced through
the different forms of the letters which developed in various parts of India
and abroad.

The earliest written records found in the area which is modern Burma are
stone inscriptions in Pali, the Indian language of the Buddhist scriptures.
Discovered at Śrī Kṣetra,[1] the capital of a people known as the Pyu,[2] the
oldest inscription dates from about A.D. 500 and contains letters which re-
semble the Kadamba script used in the third century in North Canara, near Goa
on the west coast of India. However, later inscriptions in the Pyu language,
which was not Indian but Tibeto-Burmese, also contain letters resembling the
Pallava script used at the Hinayana Buddhist center of Conjeeveram in the
area of Madras on the east coast. Thus Pyu culture was apparently influenced
by more than one Indian source over a period of time, and the Pyu writing
system emerges as a mixture of south Indian alphabets.

South of the Pyu, the dominant group was the Mon, a people closely relat-
ed to the Khmer. The Mon were centered in two areas, one along the Chaopraya
River in Thailand, the other in the Moulmein-Pegu area of lower Burma, with
a principal center at Thaton on the east coast of the Gulf of Martaban. The
oldest Mon inscription, found at Lopburi in Thailand, dates from the eighth
century and is written in the Pallava script. Since the Pyu inscriptions
antedate those of the Mon, it has been conjectured that the latter borrowed
the Pyu writing system. However, with the greater resemblance of Mon writing
to pure Pallava script, plus the fact that Thaton was itself a major Buddhist

---

1. Modern Hmawza, near Prome in central Burma.

2. Pyu is the Chinese name for this people. The "New T'ang History" records
   that they called themselves the t'u-lo-chu.

ix

center and is known to have had relations with Conjeeveram, it appears more probable that the Mon borrowed their writing system directly from India, independently of the Pyu.

Some time after A.D. 718, Śrī Kṣetra apparently fell to attackers,[3] and the Pyu moved north, establishing a new capital at Halin, north of present-day Mandalay. In A.D. 832, and again in 835, Halin was sacked by a group called the Nanchao[4] from western Yünnan. From that point, all mention of the Pyu as rulers in the area disappears; probably they were gradually assimilated into the Burmese, who were at that time migrating into central Burma and beginning to assert their dominance. The latter, apparently about A.D. 850, founded their own capital at Pagán, on the Irrawaddy River southwest of modern Mandalay, and their power and influence in the area expanded steadily thereafter. Despite extensive contact with the Pyu over the following two centuries,[5] the Burmese appear not to have adopted the latter's practice of applying an Indian alphabet to their own language. But in A.D. 1057 one of the first Burmese kings, Aniruddha, conquered Thaton and on his return to Pagán took with him the most learned monks, with their scriptures and commentaries, and the best artists and artisans of the Mon. The first inscription in Burmese dates from the following year and is written in an alphabet almost identical with that of the Mon inscriptions. Aside from the rounding of the originally square characters, this alphabet has remained largely unchanged to the present day.

Burmese, then, is written with an alphabet of considerable antiquity, borrowed indirectly from the south of India, and derived ultimately from that of Sanskrit. This workbook is a description of that writing system and its application to modern Burmese.

2.   The Sounds of Burmese.

Since the student is presumed to have had some contact with the sounds of Burmese before beginning this book, only a short summary is presented here.[6]

---

3.   Possibly Sgaw Karen.

4.   These were probably predominantly Lolo, another Tibeto-Burman people.

5.   Such contact is attested at least as late as the twelfth century, for the text of the Myazedi pagoda inscription of about 1113 is written in each of four languages: Pali, Burmese, Mon, and Pyu.

6.   For a more detailed description, see the Introduction to William S. Cornyn and D. Haigh Roop, _Beginning Burmese_ (Yale University Press, 1968).

a)   The Syllable.

A syllable in Burmese consists of an initial consonant or a cluster
of two consonants, a vowel nucleus pronounced with one of four tones or
atonically, and sometimes final /-n/. That is:

$$C_1 (C_2) \overset{(T)}{V} (n)$$

The elements that fill these syllable positions are thirty-one consonants,
nine vowels and diphthongs, and four tones.

b)   The Consonants.

Table I on the following page shows the consonants arranged phonetically by position and manner of articulation. All consonants occur initially
in a syllable, but only /n/ occurs finally.

c)   Consonant Clusters.

Besides the combinations with /h/ shown in Table I (these are included
under C_1 in the syllable diagram above), consonant clusters occur with /y/ and
/w/ in the C_2 position:

  /-y/ occurs with /p, hp, b, m, hm, n, hn/ and, rarely, with /1, hl/.

  /-w/ occurs with all initial consonants except /w/ and /q/.

d)   The Vowels.

The vocalic nuclei of Burmese syllables are the nine monophthongs and
diphthongs arranged phonetically below.

Table II - Vowels

	Front unrounded	Central unrounded	Back rounded
High	i		u
Upper mid	ei		ou
Lower mid	e		o
Low		a	
Low-to-high Diphthongs	ai		au

Table I - Consonants

	Labial	Dental	Sibilant	Palatal	Velar	Glottal
Voiceless unaspirated[7]	p	t	s	c	k	q
Voiceless aspirated[7]	hp	ht	hs	hc	hk	
Voiced unaspirated[7]	b	d	z	j	g	
Voiced nasal	m	n			ng	
Voiceless nasal	hm	hn			hng	
Semi-vowel	w			y		
Voiceless spirant		th		hy		h
Voiced spirant		dh				
Voiced lateral		l				
Voiceless lateral		hl				
Voiced flap or spirant		r[8]				

7. In the first three rows, labial, dental, velar, and glottal consonants are stops, the palatals are affricates.

8. In loan words only.

e)   The Tones.

Tone I: Low level; written /-/ within a word, unmarked before space.

Tone II: Long high falling; written /:/.

Tone III: Short high falling, slow glottal closure; written /./.

Tone IV: Short high level, sharp glottal closure; written /'/.

Atonic syllables: Short with neutral pitch; occur only with vowel /a/
                   and before another syllable; unmarked.

f)   Limitations of Occurrence.

Only certain combinations of vowels, tones, and final /-n/ occur.
These are shown in the following table. Note particularly that final /-n/
never occurs in a syllable with tone IV.

Table III - Nuclear Vowels with the Tones and Final /-n/

	Without /-n/				With /-n/		
Tones	I	II	III	IV	I	II	III
Vowels							
a	a	a:	a.	a'	an	an:	an.
i	i	i:	i.	i'	in	in:	in.
u	u	u:	u.	u'	un	un:	un.
ei	ei	ei:	ei.	ei'	ein	ein:	ein.
ou	ou	ou:	ou.	ou'	oun	oun:	oun.
e	e	e:	e.	e'			
o	o	o:	o.				
ai				ai'	ain	ain:	ain.
au				au'	aun	aun:	aun.

This book is designed to present the Burmese writing system step-by-step, with reading and writing exercises on each new element as it is introduced, so that the student will gradually build up a thorough knowledge of the symbols and the ways in which they combine. It is intended not to teach actual words, but to prepare the student for reading by providing a smooth transition from the Burmese sound system to its written representation. Once the student has worked his way through the exercises, he should be able to apply the system with relative ease to actual texts, since he will already have assimilated the symbols and their combinations.

An attempt has been made to give explanations sufficiently complete to permit the student to work through the system on his own with little or no help from an instructor; the only prerequisite is a familiarity with the sounds of Burmese. Thus it is recommended that the book be assigned <u>outside of class</u> as soon as the student has a reasonably firm grasp of the sounds, but before reading of texts is undertaken. For this purpose we have found it convenient to break the text into short sections to be assigned over a period of two or three days; for example, the first assignment might consist of pages 1-10, through question 10, the second of pages 11-19, through question 22, etc.

While the transcription used is that of Cornyn and Roop's <u>Beginning Burmese</u>, this workbook is designed to stand on its own, independent of the earlier text. The gradual introduction of the written elements, with exercises at each new step, should facilitate the student's acquisition of the Burmese writing system in any elementary course in the language.

TO THE STUDENT

This book is designed to teach you the Burmese writing system by giving you repeated opportunities to read and write forms in the language.

As you go through the material, you will find sets of questions to answer. Each set concentrates on the most recently introduced elements of the writing system, but it also includes earlier material, so that you will be continually reviewing and strengthening your control of what you have learned. Each question is followed by a blank in which you are to write your answer. Except in the periodic review tests, the correct answers are given directly below the question blanks. Cover the page you are reading with a sheet of heavy paper or cardboard and move it down, line by line. When you come to a QUESTION (regularly capitalized), write the required forms in the blanks on the first line, then move the cardboard down for an immediate check on your answers.

The review tests sum up everything you have learned at a particular point, providing periodic checks on your retention of the material. If you find that you are making a considerable number of mistakes in a review test, go back and check the trouble spots in the preceding text. Do not allow them to go unlearned, for the point you are unsure of may be just the one you need in order to understand a later combination.

CHAPTER 1

INITIAL CONSONANTS - VOWELS

A variety of elements occurs in the syllables of spoken Burmese, but
every syllable contains at least an initial consonant and a vowel. Our
introduction of the writing system begins with the symbols for these basic
elements: the thirty-three consonant symbols and the seven vowel symbols.

To start with, here is a group of five consonants known collectively
as the labials:

Symbol	Transcription	Burmese Name	Translation[1]
ပ	/p/	/pa.zau'/	steep (sided) pa
ဖ	/hp/	/hpa. qou'htou'/	capped hpa
ဗ	/b/	/ba. lahcai'/	top-indented ba
ဘ	/b/	/ba.goun:/	hump-backed ba
မ	/m/	/ma./	

ပ /pa.zau'/ "steep (sided) pa" is written in two strokes, like this:

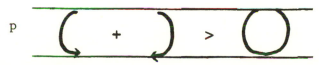

Practice writing it between the lines below as illustrated. Make your lines
as uniformly round as you can and be careful to follow the direction and
order of the strokes shown above.

ဖ /hpa. qou'htou'/ "capped hpa" starts with the same two strokes as ပ ,
then adds a third:

---

1. Each symbol has a name used for spelling and consisting, for the conson-
    ants, of the consonant sound plus /a./, usually with a word which gives
    a brief description of the symbol. For the vowels the name is a descrip-
    tion only. In presenting the symbols, the transcribed Burmese name and
    its translation are given following the symbol and its value in transcrip-
    tion.

hp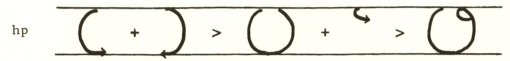

Practice writing ⊙ between the lines as you did with ʋ /pa.zau'/.

ʋ /ba. lahcai'/ "top-indented <u>ba</u>" also begins with the two strokes of ʋ but adds a different third stroke:

b

Practice writing it.

ᢍ /ba.goun:/ "hump-backed <u>ba</u>" is quite different in form; it is writ-ten in two strokes:

b

The first stroke is already the width of ʋ , with the second slightly nar-rower, so that the whole letter is almost twice the width of the other la-bials. This distinction between single- and double-width consonants is im-portant in writing, as you will see in a moment. Practice writing ᢍ in the lines below, keeping the proportions shown in the illustration.

ℊ /ma./ is single-width; it is written in two strokes:

m

Practice writing it.

QUESTION 1:   Write the values of the following consonants in transcription.
              (Don't be surprised to see an item repeated in the exercises;
              the more you are exposed to a given form, the better you will
              retain it.)

ဗ ________	မ ________	ပ ________	ဘ ________
/b/	/m/	/p/	/b/
ဖ ________	ပ ________	ဘ ________	မ ________
/hp/	/p/	/b/	/m/

QUESTION 2: Write each of the labial consonants after the sound it represents. Remember that /b/ is written in two ways.

/hp/ ____________________ /p/ ____________________

ဖ ပ

/b/ ____________________ /m/ ____________________

ဗ ဘ မ

Unlike English, Burmese is not necessarily written with a sequence of symbols progressing from left to right; some symbols are written above or below the initial consonant. For example, the symbol for the vowel /i/ is written above the consonant. This symbol is:

Symbol[2]	Transcription	Burmese Name	Translation
-ိ	/i/	/loun:ji: tin hsan hka'/	big circle put on, with a grain of rice added

It is written in one stroke:  and is the same size as ပ /pa.-zau'/. Practice writing -ိ between the lines as illustrated.

ိ

With the labial consonants, -ိ /loun:ji: tin hsan hka'/ looks like this:

ပိ /pi/ ဖိ /hpi/ ဗိ /bi/ ဘိ /bi/ မိ /mi/[3]

2. When vowel and tone symbols are cited in isolation, a hyphen indicates the position of an initial consonant.

3. These examples, like the syllables in the exercises, illustrate the manner in which symbols are combined. Not all these syllables are actual words in Burmese.

You can see that ⍩ is written directly over single-width consonants, but over the right side of double-width consonants. In each case the consonant is written first, the vowel second.

QUESTION 3: Write the following syllables in transcription.

ပိ _____   ဘိ _____   ဗိ _____   မိ _____

      /pi/   /bi/   /bi/   /mi/

ဖိ _____   ပိ _____   မိ _____   ဖိ _____

    /hpi/   /pi/   /mi/   /hpi/

QUESTION 4: Now write these syllables in Burmese. Give more than one
                 writing where possible.

/mi/ _____   /bi/ _____

          မိ   ဗိ   ဘိ

/hpi/ _____   /pi/ _____

          ဖိ   ပိ

The vowel /u/, on the other hand, is written <u>under</u> the consonant.

Symbol	Transcription	Burmese Name	Translation
‖	/u/	/hnahcaun: ngin/	two strokes drawn out

It is written: + | > ‖   and is the same height as ၀ /pa.zau'/

but narrower. Practice writing ‖ between the lines as illustrated.

‖ _____

With the labial consonants, ‖ /hnahcaun: ngin/ looks like this:

ပု /pu/   ဖု /hpu/   ဗု /bu/   ဘု /bu/   မု /mu/

The initial consonant is written first, and ‖ is written so that the right stroke is directly below the right edge of the consonant letter.

QUESTION 5: Give the values of the following syllables in transcription.
           From now on in the exercises, syllable types introduced

earlier will be included to keep them fresh in your mind.

ဘူ ______	မူ ______	ပီ ______
/bu/	/mu/	/pi/
ဗူ ______	ပူ ______	ဘီ ______
/bu/	/pu/	/bi/
ဖူ ______	မီ ______	မူ ______
/hpu/	/mi/	/mu/

QUESTION 6: What are the Burmese writings for the following syllables? Give more than one where possible.

/pu/ ______ ပူ	/hpi/ ______ ဖီ
/bu/ ______ ဗူ ဘူ	/mu/ ______ မူ
/hpu/ ______ ဖူ	/bi/ ______ ဗီ ဘီ

The vowel /ei/ is written before the initial consonant symbol, even though it is pronounced after the consonant. The symbol is:

Symbol	Transcription	Burmese Name	Translation
ေ–	/ei/	/thawei htou:/	thrust in front

It is written in one stroke:  and is the same size as ပ /pa.zau'/.

Practice writing this symbol between the lines.

ေ

With the labial consonants, ေ– /thawei htou:/ forms such syllables as:

ပေ /pei/ ဖေ /hpei/ ဗေ /bei/, etc.

Here the writing is from left to right; that is, the vowel symbol is written first.

QUESTION 7: Give the value of each of the following syllables.

ဗေ _____   ဗော _____   မေ _____

        /bei/   /bei/   /mei/

ပှု _____   ဗိ _____   ပေ _____

        /pu/   /bi/   /pei/

ဗော _____   ဗေ _____   ဖေ _____

        /bei/   /mei/   /hpei/

QUESTION 8: Give Burmese writings (as many as possible) for each of the
             following syllables.

/mei/ _____   /bu/ _____

             ဗေ   ပှု   ဖှု

/pei/ _____   /hpei/ _____

             ဗေ   ဖေ

/hpu/ _____   /pi/ _____

             ပှု   ဗိ

/bei/ _____   /mi/ _____

        ဗေ   ဗော   ဗိ

The vowel /a/ is written <u>after</u> the initial consonant letter. The symbol is:

Symbol	Transcription	Burmese Name	Translation
— ာ	/a/	/yei: hca./	(line) drawn down

It is written in one stroke: and is the same size as ပ /pa.zau'/.

Practice writing it.

ာ ____

With the labial consonants, ‑ာ /yei: hca./ forms such syllables as:

မာ /ma/ ဘာ /ba/ ဖာ /hpa/, etc.

QUESTION 9: Give the values of the following syllables.

ဗာ ________ /ba/	ပု ________ /pu/	မာ ________ /ma/
ဘာ ________ /ba/	ဘီ ________ /bi/	ဖာ ________ /hpa/
ပီ ________ /pi/	မု ________ /mu/	ဗေ ________ /bei/

QUESTION 10: Give Burmese writings for the following syllables.

/hpa/ ________ ဖာ	/hpei/ ________ ဖေ
/ba/ ________ ဗာ ဘာ	/mi/ ________ မီ
/pi/ ________ ပီ	/bu/ ________ ဗု ဘု
/ma/ ________ မာ	/pu/ ________ ပု

The next group of consonants we will consider is the dentals:

Symbol	Transcription	Burmese Name	Translation
တ	/t/	/ta. wun:bu/	pot-bellied ta
ထ	/ht/	/hta. hsin-du:/	elephant-fetter hta

Symbol	Transcription	Burmese Name	Translation
ဒ	/d/	/da.dwei:/	twisted <u>da</u>
ဓ	/d/	/da. qau'hcai'/	bottom-indented <u>da</u>
န	/n/	/na.nge/ or /na./	small <u>na</u>

တ /ta. wun:bu/ "pot-bellied <u>ta</u>" is a double-width consonant written in two strokes:

t 

The left side of တ is a circle the same size as ပ /pa.zau'/; the right side is exactly the same as that of ဗ /ba.goun:/. Practice writing တ in the lines below, keeping the proportions of the illustration.

ထ /hta. hsin-du:/ "elephant-fetter <u>hta</u>" is very similar to တ /ta. wun:bu/; the second stroke is merely extended a little to meet the initial stroke. This consonant is written:

ht 

Practice it.

ဒ /da.dwei:/ "twisted <u>da</u>" is a single-width consonant written in one stroke from the top:

d 

Practice it.

ဓ /da. qau'hcai'/ "bottom-indented <u>da</u>" looks like, and is written in the same way as, the vowel symbol ီ /loun:ji: tin hsan hka'/, but it is written on a line with the other consonants, not above them. Practice writing ဓ between the lines.

ၕ /na.nge/ "small <u>na</u>" (or simply /na./) is a single-width consonant, but it differs from other letters you have learned in having a tail that extends lower. It is written in one stroke, starting from the top:

n

Practice writing it.

These consonant letters combine with the vowel symbols you have learned in the same way as the labials. For example:

တိ /ti/   ထု /htu/   ဒိ /di/

ဒေ /dei/   နာ /na/   ၕု /nu/

When ၕ /na.nge/ occurs with ꜜ /hnahcaun: ngin/, the tail of the consonant is either shortened, as above, or slanted to the right: ၕ .

QUESTION 11: Give the values of the following syllables.

ဒု _____   ၕိ _____   ဒေ _____
        /du/   /ni/   /pei/

တာ _____   ထိ _____   နာ _____
        /ta/   /hti/   /na/

ရု _____   ဒေ _____   ထာ _____
        /du/   /tei/   /hta/

QUESTION 12: Give Burmese writings for the following syllables.

/ti/ _____   /ta/ _____

                တိ   ထာ

/dei/ _____   /bu/ _____

        ဒေ   ဒေ   ရု   ၕု

/na/ _____   /mu/ _____

                  ၛၢ   ၛ

/di/ _____   /nu/ _____

            ၘိ   ၘ   နို

/htei/ _____   /hpa/ _____

                  ေထ   ဖ

The vowel /e/ is written above the initial consonant in the same position as ၘ /loun:ji: tin hsan hka'/. The symbol for /e/ is:

       Symbol   Transcription   Burmese Name   Translation
         ⌣   /e:/   /nau' pyi'/   thrown backwards

You may have noticed that all our syllables so far have been in tone I. Each
vowel symbol represents a tone as well as a vowel quality, and the first four
vowels you have learned all represent tone I.

            UNLIKE THE EARLIER VOWEL SYMBOLS, ⌣ REPRESENTS
                        TONE II, NOT TONE I.

/nau' pyi'/ is written: and combines with the consonants to

form such syllables as:

        ထဲ /hte:/   နဲ /ne:/   ဘဲ /be:/, etc.

Again, like ၘ /loun:ji: tin hsan hka'/, ⌣ /nau' pyi'/ is written directly
over single-width consonants but over the right side of double-width consonants.
QUESTION 13: What tone is associated with ⌣ /nau' pyi'/?

              _____

                        /:/ Tone II

    What tone is associated with the other vowel symbols you have
    learned?

/-/   Tone I

QUESTION 14:   Give the values of the following syllables. Pay particular
attention to the tones.

ဗဲ _____   ဒဲ _____   တဲ _____
      /me:/   /de:/   /te:/

တေ _____   ပဲ _____   ဘိ _____
      /tei/   /pe:/   /bi/

 နု _____   နဲ _____   ထဲ _____
      /nu/   /ne:/   /hte:/

QUESTION 15:   Give Burmese writings for the following syllables.

/be:/ _____   /nei/ _____

            ဗဲ   ဘဲ   နေ

/pe:/ _____   /mi/ _____

               ပဲ   မိ

/ne:/ _____   /de:/ _____

               နဲ   ဒဲ   ဗဲ

/hpei/ _____   /hte:/ _____

            ဖေ   ထဲ

You have learned that the vowel /i/ is represented with ◌ိ /loun: ji: tin
hsan hka'/. But /loun: ji: tin/ "big circle put on" also occurs without /hsan
hka'/ "the grain of rice added." It then has the value /i./.

Symbol	Transcription	Burmese Name	Translation
◌ိ	/i./	/loun: ji: tin/	big circle put on

ိ THUS REPRESENTS TONE III WITH /i/, JUST AS

ဲ REPRESENTS TONE II WITH /e/.

/loun:ji: tin/ is written:  and combines with the consonants in the same way as ီ /loun:ji: tin hsan hka'/. For example:

ဒိ /di./ ဗိ /bi./, etc.

QUESTION 16: Give the values of the following syllables.

တိ ________	နိ ________	ဒီ ________
/ti./	/ni./	/di/
ဘဲ ________	မိ ________	ဗာ ________
/be:/	/mi./	/ba/
ပိ ________	ဒေ ________	ဖီ ________
/pi./	/dei/	/hpi/

Similarly, you have learned that /u/ is represented with ူ /hnahcaun: ngin/ "two strokes drawn out." However, "one stroke drawn out" also occurs, representing /u./ - tone III:

Symbol	Transcription	Burmese Name	Translation
ု	/u./	/tahcaun: ngin/	one stroke drawn out

It is written:  and combines with the consonants in the same position as ူ /hnahcaun: ngin/. For example:

မု /mu./ ထု /htu./, etc.

QUESTION 17: Give the values of the following syllables.

နု ________	တု ________	ထိ ________
/nu./	/tu./	/hti./

မိ _____   ရု _____   ဘူ _____
        /mi/   /bu/   /bu./

ဒေ _____   ဒု _____   ဖု _____
        /de:/   /du./   /hpu./

As the symbols for /i/ and /u/ in tone III contain one less stroke than
the tone I symbols, so /a./ is written with one less stroke than /a/; that is,
—ာ /yei: hca./ drops entirely. Tone III /a/ is represented with the consonant standing alone, as in the names of the letters. For example:

    ပ /pa./   တ /ta./   န /na./, etc.

QUESTION 18: Give the values of the following syllables.

မ _____   တာ _____   ဘ _____
        /ma./   /ta/   /ba./

ရု _____   ထေ _____   ဖ _____
        /pu./   /htei/   /hpa./

နိ _____   ဘာ _____   ဒူ _____
        /ni/   /ba/   /du/

ဒ _____   တိ _____   ဖေ _____
        /da./   /ti./   /hpe:/

QUESTION 19: Give Burmese writings for the following syllables. Give more
              than one writing where possible and take particular care with
              the tones.

/ba./ _____   /hti/ _____

            ဗ   ဘ   တိ

/mu./ _____   /hpa/ _____

            ရု   ဖာ

/na./ _____   /mi./ _____

                        ၆   ၌

/de:/ _____   /ta./ _____

                   ဒ   ၆   တ

/hpei/ _____   /pa./ _____

                   ၆ဗ   ပ

QUESTION 20: Write as many symbols as you can for each of the following
              vowels and indicate the tone of each symbol after it.

/i/ _____

/u/ _____

/a/ _____

/ei/ _____

/e/ _____

                /i/ -   ၐ   tone I   ၐ   tone III
                /u/ -   ၞ   tone I   ၞ   tone III
                /a/ -   — ၁   tone I   —   [zero] tone III
                /ei/ -   ၆ —   tone I
                /e/ -   ၚ   tone II

The next group of consonants we will refer to as the <u>palatals</u>:[4]

    Symbol   Transcription   Burmese Name   Translation

       စ   /s/   /sa.loun:/   round <u>sa</u>

       ဆ   /hs/   /hsa.lein/   twisted <u>hsa</u>

---

4. This is a convenient cover term taken from the class of these letters in
    the Indian alphabet from which they were borrowed. In modern Burmese only
    /nya./ retains the palatal pronunciation.

Symbol	Transcription	Burmese Name	Translation
ဇ	/z/	/za.gwe:/	split za
ဈ	/z/	/za. myin-zwe:/	bridle za
ည	/ny/	/nya./	

ဝ /sa.loun:/ "round sa" is a single-width letter written in either of two ways, each using one stroke:

Practice writing it.

_____
ⓢ _____

ဆ /hsa.lein/ "twisted hsa" is double-width and is written in two strokes:

Practice writing it.

_____
ဆ _____

ဇ /za.gwe:/ "split za" is written in one stroke and is essentially a single-width consonant, but the upper tail extends slightly beyond normal single width.

Practice writing ဇ .

_____
ဇ _____

ဈ /za. myin-zwe:/ "bridle za" is also essentially a single-width consonant, but the right side extends slightly beyond single width. This letter is written in two strokes, the first of which is ဝ /sa.loun:/:

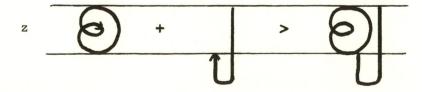

Practice writing ရ .

    The last of the palatals is ည /nya./. It is a double-width letter
written in two strokes:

ny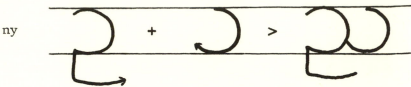

As shown, the tail of the handwritten form extends only half the width of
the letter, but in the printed form the tail extends the entire width.
Practice writing ည .

    You should have no difficulty now in combining these consonants with
the vowel symbols in the following exercises.

QUESTION 21: Give the values of the following syllables.

ရု _____   ညာ _____   ေဇ _____
       /su./   /nya/   /ze:/

ေရ _____   စိ _____   ေတ _____
       /zei/   /si./   /tei/

ဆ _____   ညီ _____   ဆု _____
       /hsa./   /nyi/   /hsu/

QUESTION 22: Give Burmese writings for the following syllables.

/nya./ _____   /za/ _____
         ည   ဇာ   ဆာ

/me:/ _____   /hsei/ _____
        ေမ   ေဆ

/si./ _____   /nye:/ _____
        စိ   ညဲ

/zi/ _____   /hpu/ _____

     ဇိ ဇ္ရ   ဖူ

/hsu./ _____   /sa./ _____

      ဆူ   စ

The vowels /o/ and /ou/ are represented with combinations of symbols you have already learned.

Symbol	Transcription	Burmese Name
ေ ―ာ	/o:/	/thawei htou:, yei: hca./
◌ု	/ou/	/loun: ji: tin, tahcaun: ngin/

Again, each represents a tone as well as a vowel quality: ေ ―ာ is tone II, ◌ု tone I. The symbols are written in the same way in these combinations as when they are used separately:

ေဘာ /bo:/ ေနာ /no:/ တု /tou/ ဆု /sou/

QUESTION 23: Give the values of the following syllables.

ဆု _____   ေထာ _____   ပု _____

  /hsou/   /to:/   /pou/

ေမာ _____   သိ _____   ဒု _____

  /mo:/   /si./   /du./

ဘု _____   ေထ _____   ညာ _____

  /bou/   /htei/   /nya/

ေဆာ _____   တု _____   ေဖာ _____

  /hso:/   /bou/   /hpo:/

In writing syllables with these combinations, the order is:

  with ေ ―ာ - first ေ ― /thawei htou:/, then the initial consonant, then ―ာ /yei: hca./.

  with ◌ု - first the initial consonant, then ◌ု /tahcaun: ngin/, then ◌ု /loun: ji: tin/.

QUESTION 24: Give Burmese writings for the following syllables.

/mo:/ _____   /hso:/ _____

              မော   ဆော

/sei/ _____   /dou/ _____

              စေ   ဒို   ဒို

/nya/ _____   /no:/ _____

              ညာ   နော

/hti./ _____   /zo:/ _____

              ဌိ   ဇော   ဇျော

/sou/ _____   /hpou/ _____

              စို   ဖို

The next group of consonants is the <u>velars</u>:

Symbol	Transcription	Burmese Name	Translation
က	/k/	/ka.ji:/	great <u>ka</u>
ခ	/hk/	/hka.gwei:/	curved <u>hka</u>
ဂ	/g/	/ga.nge/	small <u>ga</u>
ဃ	/g/	/ga.ji:/	great <u>ga</u>
င	/ng/	/nga./	

က /ka.ji:/ "great <u>ka</u>" is double-width and is written in two strokes:

Practice writing it.

    ခ /hka.gwei:/ "curved <u>hka</u>" is like the left side of ဆ /hsa.lein/. It is single-width and is written:

hk

Practice writing it.

ဥ _____

ဂ   /ga.nge/ "small ga" is like the first half of ကာ /ka.ji:/:

g   Practice it. ဂ _____

ဃ   /ga.ji:/ "great ga" is double-width and is written in three strokes:

g   (+) > ◯ +) > ◯◯

Practice writing it.

ဃ _____

င   /nga./ is written in one stroke:

ng   Practice it. င _____

QUESTION 25: Give the values of the following syllables.

ခု _____	ဂေ _____	တိ _____
/hku./	/gei/	/ti./
ကာ _____	ဆော _____	ငို _____
/ka/	/so:/	/ngou/
ဂဲ _____	ပေ _____	ဆိ _____
/ge:/	/pei/	/hsi/
င _____	ခို _____	ကို _____
/nga./	/hkou/	/kou/

QUESTION 26: Give Burmese writings for the following syllables.

/gu/ _____   /hke:/ _____

ကူ   ဂူ   ခဲ

/na/ _____   /bi./ _____

နာ   ဗိ   ဘိ

/ga./ _____   /ngu./ _____

ဂ   ဃ   ငု

/ko:/ _____   /hkei/ _____

ကော   ခေ

We call the next group of consonants the <u>Pali dentals</u> because they are pronounced like the dental consonant group you have learned (/t/, /d/, etc.) but appear almost entirely in loan words from the Pali language. They are much less common than the dentals you already know.

Symbol	Transcription	Burmese Name	Translation
ဋ	/t/	/ta. talin:jei'/	bier-hook <u>ta</u>
ဌ	/ht/	/hta. wun:be:/	duck <u>hta</u>
ဍ	/d/	/da. yin-gau'/	crooked breasted <u>da</u>
ဎ	/d/	/da. yei-hmou'/	water dipper <u>da</u>
ဏ	/n/	/na.ji:/	great <u>na</u>

These are written:

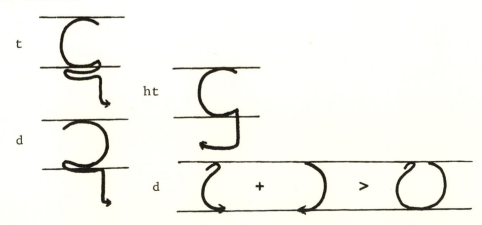

n

Practice writing these consonants below, keeping in mind the different widths and the tails which extend below the lower line.

QUESTION 27:   Give the values of the following syllables.

ဒိ _____	ကူ _____	ထေ _____
/ti/	/ku/	/htei/

ကူ _____	ဒေ _____	ထာ _____
/nu./	/dei/	/hta/

ဎ _____	ဒိ _____	တော _____
/da./	/di./	/to:/

ထော _____	ကို _____	ဒိ _____
/to:/	/nou/	/di/

QUESTION 28:   Give Burmese writings for the following syllables.

/ta/ _____   /hpo:/ _____

          တာ   ထာ   ဖော

/htei/ _____   /di/ _____

          ထေ   ဒေ   ဒိ   ဒိ   ဒိ   ဒိ

/hse:/ _____   /nu/ _____

                    ဆဲ   ရိ   ကျို

/gou/ _____   /dei/ _____

                ရို   သို့   ေဒ   ေမ   ေဍ   ေပ

/hta/ _____   /to:/ _____

            ထာ   ဌာ   ေတာ   ေဍာ

You have already learned that certain sounds are written with more than
one letter (/t/ with ထ and ဋ , /b/ with ဘ and ဗ , etc.). There remain two
other initial consonant sounds that have multiple representation; they are
/y/ and /l/, and the writings are:

Symbol	Transcription	Burmese Name	Translation
ယ	/y/	/ya. pale'/	supine <u>ya</u>
ရ	/y/	/ya.gau'/	crooked <u>ya</u>
လ	/l/	/la./	
ဠ	/l/	/la.ji:/	great <u>la</u>

For /y/, both ယ /ya. pale'/ "supine <u>ya</u>" and ရ /ya.gau'/ "crooked <u>ya</u>" are very
common, but for /l/, လ /la./ occurs far more commonly than ဠ /la.ji:/ "great
<u>la</u>." The last is like the Pali dentals; it appears almost entirely in loan
words from the Pali language.

These four letters are written:

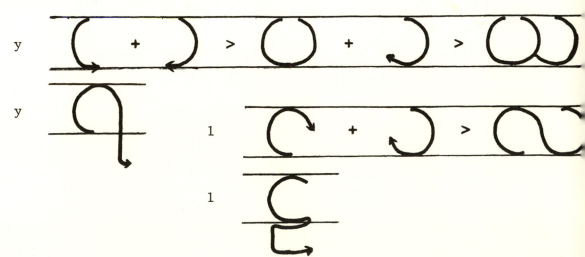

Practice writing them.

ဃ

ဌ

ဏ

ဉ

    The following four miscellaneous letters complete the list of initial
consonants:

Symbol	Transcription	Burmese Name
၀	/w/	/wa./
သ	/th/	/tha./
ဟ	/h/	/ha./
အ	/q/	/qa./

They are written:

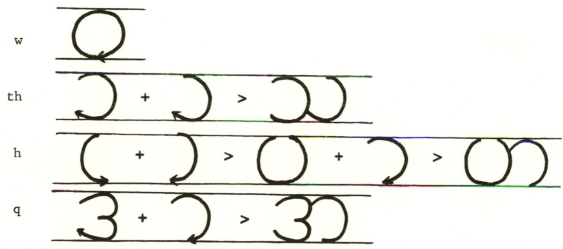

Practice writing them.

၀

သ

ဟ

အ

QUESTION 29:   Give the values of the following syllables.

သိ _____   ယု _____   ေဝ _____

        /thi./   /yu/   /wei/

လီ _____   ေဟာ _____   ရု _____

        /li/   /ho:/   /yu./

ယာ _____   လို _____   လ _____

        /ya/   /lou/   /la./

ဲအ _____   ဟို _____   ေသာ _____

        /qe:/   /hou/   /tho:/

ဝိ _____   ေရ _____   ေအ _____

        /wi./   /ye:/   /qei/

QUESTION 30:   Write the following syllables in Burmese.

/you/ _____   /ha/ _____

        လို ရု   ဟာ

/wi./ _____   /hte:/ _____

          ဝိ   ထဲ ၄

/lei/ _____   /qu./ _____

        ေလ ၄ဲ   အု

/thi/ _____   /la./ _____

          သိ   လ ၄

/we:/ _____   /yo:/ _____

          ဝဲ   ေယာ ေရာ

/qa/ _____   /thu/ _____

               အာ   သူ

You have learned the symbol ─ာ /yei: hca./ for the vowel /a/ in tone I,
but with certain consonants the use of this symbol could cause confusion. For
example: ဝ /wa./ + ာ to form the syllable /wa/, would give the written form
ဝာ, which looks like ထ /ta. wun:bu/. Similarly, ဂ /ga.nge/ + ာ for /ga/
would result in the form ဂာ , which looks like ကာ /ka.ji:/. Such confusion
is avoided by using a long form of /yei: hca./ with certain of the single-
width consonants.

This form is written:

In combination with initial consonant symbols it looks like this:

         ပါ /pa/   ဂါ /ga/   ဝါ /wa/, etc.

This long form also occurs with ေ─ /thawei htou:/ in the combination ေ─ါ
/o:/. For example:

         ပေါ /po:/   ငေါ /ngo:/, etc.

The long form of /yei: hca./ is <u>regularly</u> written with ခ , ဂ , င , ဒ ,
ပ , and ဝ . It is sometimes also written with ဃ , ဆ , ဓ , and ဟ .

QUESTION 31:   Give Burmese writings for the following syllables. Use the
               long form of /yei: hca./ only with those consonants with which
               it regularly occurs.

/nga/ _____   /hko:/ _____

               ငါ   ခေါ

/ma/ _____   /da/ _____

               မာ   ဒါ ဓာ ဒ္ဓာ ထာ

/sa/ _____   /hpo:/ _____

               စာ   ဖော

/go:/ ____________________ /wa/ ____________________

ဂေါ ဃော ဝါ

/po:/ ____________________ /ba/ ____________________

ပေါ ဗာ ဘာ

/no:/ ____________________ /ngo:/ ____________________

နော ဏော ငေါ

Certain consonant letters with tails that extend below the line occupy the space in which ◌ု /tahcaun: ngin/ and ◌ူ /hnahcaun: ngin/ are normally written. These are:

ဈ , ဍ , ဌ , ဋ , and ဠ

When /u/, /u./, or /ou/ occurs with one of these consonants, ◌ု or ◌ူ is lengthened and written to the right of the consonant:

ဈူ /zu/ ဌူ /htu/ ဠု /lu./ ဍို /dou/, etc.

In typewriting, the long forms are also used with ည /nya./. In your own writing you need not worry about this -- the tail of ည is short and there is room for the short forms ◌ူ and ◌ု -- but in reading you will see such forms as: ညူ /nyu/ and ညို /nyou/.

QUESTION 32: Give Burmese writings for the following syllables.

/tu/ ____________________ /zou/ ____________________

တူ ဋူ ဇို ဈို

/yu./ ____________________ /hka/ ____________________

ယု ရု ခါ

/dou/ ____________________ /lu./ ____________________

ဒို ဓို ဍို ဎို လု ဠု

/ngo:/ _____   /htu./ _____

          ၐေါ်   ထု   ထူ

/nyou/ _____   /tou/ _____

        ညို (typed ညို)   ထို   ထို

/zu/ _____   /lou/ _____

          ရ   ရှ   လို   လို

SUMMARY:

You have now learned all thirty-three consonant letters and the seven
basic vowel symbols with their variant forms, but they have not been presented in alphabetical order. Here are the consonant symbols in a chart which
shows that order.

INITIAL CONSONANTS IN ALPHABETICAL ORDER

Velars	က	k	ခ	hk	ဂ	g	ဃ	g	င	ng
Palatals	စ	s	ဆ	hs	ဇ	z	ဈ	z	ည	ny
Pali Dentals	ဋ	t	ဌ	ht	ဍ	d	ဎ	d	ண	n
Dentals	တ	t	ထ	ht	ဒ	d	ဓ	d	န	n
Labials	ပ	p	ဖ	hp	ဗ	b	ဘ	b	မ	m
Miscellaneous	ယ	y	ရ	y	လ	l	ဝ	w	သ	th
			ဟ	h	ဠ	l	အ	q		

On the following page is a list of the vowel symbols you have learned,
including variants and combinations, in their usual alphabetical order.

[no symbol]   /a./

－ꜗ (－ꜟ)   /a/

ᴏ̲   /i./

ᴏ̱   /i/

ᅮ̲ (－ᅵ)   /u./

ᅲ̲ (－ᅵᅵ)   /u/

ᦞ －   /ei/

ꜛ   /e:/

ᦞ － ꜗ (ᦞ －ꜟ) /o:/

ᅩ̲ (ᅩᅵ)   /ou/

On the following pages you will find a review test of all the material
in this chapter. The answers this time are not mixed in with the questions,
but are given separately on the pages following the test. If you have trouble
answering the test questions, you should go back and review the chapter before
going on. The syllables presented in the following chapters are largely built
up from the basic types already described. If you are not thoroughly familiar
with the material in Chapter 1, you do not have the necessary basis for under-
standing much of what follows.

REVIEW TEST 1.

SECTION A: Give the values of the following syllables.

1.	ဆာ ____	2.	ချူ ____	3.	ဖော ____
4.	ရိ ____	5.	ဟို ____	6.	က ____
7.	ဗိ ____	8.	တူ ____	9.	ဝို ____
10.	ယေ ____	11.	အဲ ____	12.	ဌော ____
13.	ဈူ ____	14.	ပါ ____	15.	ငို ____
16.	တာ ____	17.	ဝိ ____	18.	ဋူ ____
19.	ဂေ ____	20.	ဇို ____	21.	နော ____
22.	ဘာ ____	23.	သု ____	24.	ငဲ ____
25.	ညော ____	26.	ဋို ____	27.	ထု ____
28.	မဲ ____	29.	ဝေ ____	30.	ခေါ ____
31.	ဗီ ____	32.	လာ ____	33.	ကူ ____
34.	ဆေ ____	35.	ပ ____	36.	ဖု ____
37.	သိ ____	38.	ရု ____	39.	ဒေါ ____
40.	ဖူ ____	41.	အီ ____	42.	ကိ ____
43.	ထဲ ____	44.	ဘေ ____	45.	လို ____
46.	ဟ ____	47.	ခု ____	48.	ပိ ____
49.	ညဲ ____	50.	ဒို ____	51.	ယော ____

52.   ပ္ဌ _____   53. ၍ _____   54. ဪ _____

SECTION B: Write the following syllables in Burmese.

1. /si./ _____   2. /dei/ _____

3. /ko:/ _____   4. /bu/ _____

5. /ta/ _____   6. /nyi/ _____

7. /me:/ _____   8. /you/ _____

9. /gu./ _____   10. /la./ _____

11. /ho:/ _____   12. /di/ _____

13. /za/ _____   14. /nge:/ _____

15. /hti./ _____   16. /gou/ _____

17. /hsu/ _____   18. /thou/ _____

19. /na./ _____   20. /wa/ _____

21. /pou/ _____   22. /hko:/ _____

23. /ku./ _____   24. /sa/ _____

25. /lei/ _____   26. /ta./ _____

27. /hpu/ _____   28. /hei/ _____

29. /nou/ _____   30. /hka/ _____

31. /po:/ _____   32. /zu/ _____

33. /mu./ _____   34. /hte:/ _____

35. /thi/ _____   36. /go:/ _____

37. /bou/ _____   38. /ya/ _____

39. /thu./ _____   40. /nga/ _____

41. /qe:/ _____   42. /hsei/ _____

43. /wi/ _____   44. /hpa./ _____

45. /nyo:/ _____

REVIEW TEST 1: ANSWERS.

SECTION A:

1. /hsa/	2. /du/	3. /hpo:/
4. /yi/	5. /hou/	6. /ka./
7. /si/	8. /tu/	9. /bou/
10. /yei/	11. /qe:/	12. /to:/
13. /zu/	14. /pa/	15. /ngou/
16. /ta/	17. /wi./	18. /lu./
19. /gei/	20. /zou/	21. /no:/
22. /ba/	23. /thu./	24. /nge:/
25. /nyo:/	26. /htou/	27. /htu./
28. /me:/	29. /wei/	30. /hko:/
31. /di/	32. /la/	33. /ku/
34. /hsei/	35. /da./	36. /hpu./
37. /thi./	38. /su./	39. /do:/
40. /mu/	41. /qi/	42. /ni./
43. /hte:/	44. /bei/	45. /lou/
46. /ha./	47. /hku./	48. /pi./
49. /nye:/	50. /dou/	51. /yo:/
52. /yu/	53. /na./	54. /gou/

SECTION B:

1. ဝိ	2. ဒေ ဓေ ဍေ ဎေ
3. ကော	4. ဗူ ဘူ
5. တာ ဋာ	6. ညီ
7. မဲ	8. ယို ရို
9. ဂူ ဃူ	10. လ ဠ
11. ဟော	12. ဒီ ဓီ ဍီ ဎီ

13. ဇာ ဈာ	14. ငဲ
15. ထိ ဌိ	16. ဂို ဃို
17. ဆူ	18. သို
19. န ဏ	20. ဝါ
21. ပို	22. ခေါ
23. ကူ	24. စာ
25. လေ ဠေ	26. တ ဋ
27. ဖူ	28. ဟေ
29. ဒို ဓို	30. ခါ
31. ပေါ	32. ဇူ ဈူ
33. မူ	34. ထဲ ဌဲ
35. သီ	36. ဂေါ ဃော
37. ဗို ဘို	38. ယာ ရာ
39. ဘူ	40. ငါ
41. အဲ	42. ဆေ
43. ဗီ	44. ဖ

45. ညော

CHAPTER 2

INITIAL CONSONANT CLUSTERS

In the transcription, /y/, /w/, and /h/ combine with other consonants to
form syllable-initial clusters. Some of these are written with a single symbol in Burmese -- ∞ /ht/, သ /th/, ည /ny/, etc. -- but many are written with
a combination of an initial consonant letter and one or more of a set of four
new symbols called medials.

With the exception of ည /ny/, /y/ following another consonant is written
with one of the two following symbols:

Symbol	Transcription	Burmese Name	Translation
⫟	/-y/	/ya. pin./	supporting <u>ya</u>
ြ	/-y/	/ya. yi'/	encircling <u>ya</u>

/ya. pin./ is written: /ya. yi'/:

⫟ begins to the right of the initial consonant symbol, level with the top of
it, and ends under the right side of the consonant. ြ begins under the right
edge of the consonant symbol and circles the left side of it. Both are written immediately after the initial consonant, before vowel symbols except
/thawei htou:/. Practice writing them with the labial consonants as illustrated.

These two medials occur very commonly with the labial consonants (ပ ,
ဖ , ဗ , ဘ , မ) in such combinations as:

      ပျ /pya./   ဖျာ /hpya/   ဗျ /bye:/   မြေ /myei/

They also commonly occur with velar consonants, but these combinations have special pronunciations:

$$ ကျ \text{ or } ကြ \quad = \text{/c/} $$

$$ ချ \text{ or } ခြ \quad = \text{/hc/} $$

$$ ဂျ \text{ or } ဂြ \quad = \text{/j/} $$

ဃ /ga.ji:/ does not occur with either of these medials, but င /nga./ combines with ြ /ya. yi'/:

$$ ငြ \quad = \text{/ny/} $$

This last combination, which equals the single symbol ည /nya./, is rare.
In the following exercises you will be expected to read it, but you need not
write it when you are asked to produce the /ny/ cluster. Note that င is
unlike က , ခ , and ဂ in that it occurs only with ြ /ya. yi'/, not with
ျ /ya. pin./.

     Here are some examples of these combinations in syllables:

   ချေ /hce:/   ဂျိ /ji/   ကျာ /ca/   ငြိ /nyi./

ျ /ya. pin./ and ြ /ya. yi'/ do not normally occur with other initial consonant symbols.

     Now let us go back over these points.
QUESTION 33: a) With what consonant letters do ျ /ya. pin./ and ြ /ya.
                  yi'/ occur?

                    ပ , ဖ , ဗ , က , ဘ , ခ , ဂ , ဂ , င

     b) What initial consonant sounds are represented by

   ကြ _____?   ချ _____?   ဂျ _____?

   ြပ _____?   ချ _____?   ငြ _____?

              /c/, /my/, /j/

              /py/, /hc/, /ny/

     Another important fact to remember in connection with the /y/ medials is
that when either is present in a syllable, the long form of /yei: hca./, ျ ,
is not used. Since the medial clearly marks the right side of the initial

consonant, no confusion arises in such syllables as to whether ၁ is a vowel
symbol or part of the consonant. For example, compare the syllables ကြ /ca./
and ၮ /ja/. In the first, ြ /ya. yi'/ encloses the element ၁ , marking it
as part of the consonant က /ka.ji:/; but in the second, the position of ြ
shows that the initial consonant is ဂ /ga.nge/, while ၁ , standing outside
the medial symbol, is to be read as /yei: hca./. Thus there are such contrasts
as:

ခါ /hka/ with the long form, but:

ချာ or ၌ /hca/ with the short form

ပေါ /po:/ with the long form, but:

ပြော or ၌ /pyo:/ with the short form.

QUESTION 34: Now give the values of the following syllables.

ပြာ _____	ကြ _____	၌ _____
/bya/	/ca./	/hcei/
၌ _____	၌ _____	၌ _____
/mye:/	/pyo:/	/byi/
၌ _____	၌ _____	ချာ _____
/hpyei/	/byi./	/hca/
ကြ _____	၌ _____	၌ _____
/ca./	/nye:/	/jo:/

The long forms ◌ၟ /tahcaun: ngin/ and ◌ၠ /hnahcaun: ngin/ are written
in syllables with the /y/ medials:

ၿ /hpyu/   ကၿ /cu./   ၌ /pyu./   ၌ /hcu/

Similarly in the combination ◌ :

၌ /hcou/   ၌ /myou/

QUESTION 35: Write the following syllables in Burmese.

/cou/ _____   /pyo:/ _____

         ကျို   ကြို   ပျော   ပြော

/ja/ _____   /hci/ _____

         ဂျာ   ဂြာ   ချိ   ခြိ

/hpyu./ _____   /myi./ _____

         ဖျု   ဖြု   မျိ   မြိ

/pya./ _____   /ce:/ _____

         ပျ   ပြ   ကျဲ   ကြဲ

/byou/ _____   /hko:/ _____

     ဗျို   ဘျို   ဗြို   ဘြို   ခေါ

/hco:/ _____   /myu/ _____

      ချော   ခြော   မျု   မြု

In printing, the <u>short</u> forms ◌ and ◌ are normally used with ◌ /ya.
yi'/. In your writing you need not worry about this -- just use the long
forms regularly -- but in reading you should expect such forms as:

            ပျု /pyu./   ဖျု /hpyu/

Following an initial consonant, /w/ is represented with:

Symbol	Transcription	Burmese Name	Translation
◌	/-w/	/wa. hswe:/	suspended <u>wa</u>

Examples are:

      သွာ /thwa/   တွဲ /twe:/   မွေ /mwei/

      _____

/wa. hswe:/ is written:

            ◯⟶

It occurs directly beneath single-width consonants but below the right side
of double-width consonants. It is written immediately after the initial consonant but before vowel symbols except ၄ — /thawei htou:/. Practice writing
it with different consonants as illustrated.

When ◌ွ /wa. hswe:/ occurs with န /na.nge/ or ရ /ya.gau'/, the tail of
the consonant symbol is frequently shortened or shifted:

$$ \text{နွ} \quad or \quad \text{နွ} \quad /nwe:/ $$

$$ \text{ရွာ} \quad or \quad \text{ရွာ} \quad /ywa/ $$

Those consonants normally written with the long form of /yei: hca./ (—ှ)
occur with either the long or short form when ◌ွ /wa. hswe:/ is present:

$$ \text{ခွှ} \quad or \quad \text{ခွာ} \quad /hkwa/ \qquad\qquad \text{ပွ} \quad or \quad \text{ပွာ} \quad /pwa/, \text{ etc.} $$

QUESTION 36:   Give the values of the following syllables.

ခွှ _____   ဆွ _____   ဖွ _____

        /hkwa/   /hswe:/   /hpwe:/

မွာ _____   ထွိ _____   ယွာ _____

        /mwa/   /htwi/   /ywa/

လွဲ _____   ဂွေ _____   ဒွေ _____

        /lwe:/   /gwei/   /dwei/

ရွာ _____   ကွဲ _____   သွေ _____

        /ywa/   /kwe:/   /thwei/

QUESTION 37:   Write the following syllables in Burmese. From this point on,
               ဃ /ga.ji:/, ဠ /la.ji:/, and the Pali dentals ဍ , ဎ , ဏ ,
               ဝ , ထ , all of which occur infrequently, will be required only
               for recognition; you need not write them when giving Burmese
               forms. They do not, in any case, occur with the medials.

/ngwa/ _____   /ca/ _____

ငွီ   ငွာ   ကျာ   ကြာ

/ywe:/ _____   /hswei/ _____

ရွဲ   ရွ   ဆွေ

/thwe:/ _____   /hcou/ _____

သွဲ   ချို   ဴြို

/cu./ _____   /lwa/ _____

ကျု   ကြူ   လွာ

/myi./ _____   /nwe:/ _____

မို   ဴြို   နွဲ

/h/, when combined with the nasals /ng/, /ny/, /n/, /m/, or with /y/, /l/, or, rarely, /w/, is written:

Symbol	Transcription	Burmese Name	Translation
ှ	/h-/	/ha. htou:/	thrust-in ha

Remember that /h/ in the combinations /hk/, /hc/, /hs/, /ht/, and /hp/ is included in the Burmese initial consonant letter. ှ /ha. htou:/ occurs only with the nasals and with initial /y/, /l/, and /w/.

It is written: ┬ as in:

ငှ /hnga/   ရှိ /hyi./   လှူ /hlu/[1]   နှေ /hnei/

Practice writing /ha. htou:/ with the consonants illustrated.

ငှ ညှ နှ မှ ယှ လှ ရှ ဝှ _____

_____

_____

1. Occasionally you will also see the long forms ┐ and ┐┐ with ှ , e.g. လှ္ခ, but you should use the short forms in your own writing.

QUESTION 38: Give the values of the following syllables.

ရှေ ______	ယှာ ______	ငှို ______
/hyei/	/hya/	/hngou/
ဆွှာ ______	မှိ ______	ညှို ______
/hswa/	/hmi/	/hnyou/
လှု ______	နှော ______	ရှိ ______
/hlu./	/hno:/	/hyi./

QUESTION 39: Write the following syllables in Burmese.

/hnou/ ______	/hmu/ ______
နှို	မှု
/hla./ ______	/ywa/ ______
လှ	ယွှာ ရွှာ
/hka./ ______	/hle:/ ______
ခ	လှဲ
/hcei/ ______	/hyei/ ______
ချေ ခြေ	ယှေ ရှေ
/hnga/ ______	/hnyo:/ ______
ငှါ	ညှော

/ha. htou:/ also occurs in combination with ွ /wa. hswe:/, where interference is avoided by writing /ha. htou:/ diagonally:

as in:

မွှာ /hmwa/ နွှေ /hnwei/ လွှဲ /hlwe:/

But typewriters have only the diagonal form of /ha. htou:/, and this is used in all contexts, whether ွ /wa. hswe:/ is present or not. For the remainder of this book you will see the vertical /ha. htou:/ (ှ) only in the few cases where it is hand written. In your own writing you should, of course, use the vertical form except with ွ /wa. hswe:/.

Other combinations of medial symbols also occur, as, for example:

ကျွေ /cwei/ ခြွ /hcwa./ မြှူ /hmyu/

In such combinations, the order of writing is:

ွ /wa. hswe:/ before ှ /ha. htou:/ before { ျ /ya. pin./ or ြ /ya. yi'/ }

Below are the other combinations which occur; some of these present further problems of interference between symbols.

ွ + ျ ; ျ is shortened:

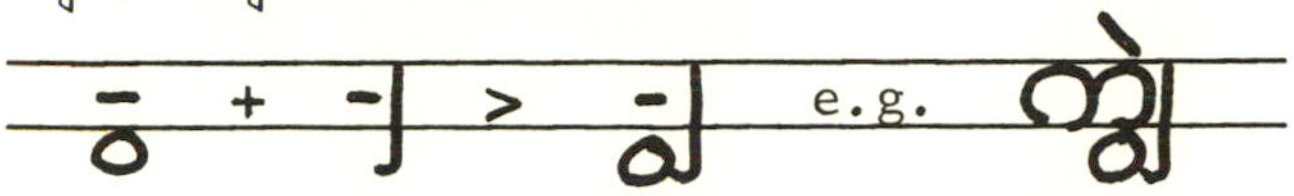

typed ကျွဲ /cwe:/

ွ + ြ ; ြ starts from the bottom of ွ :

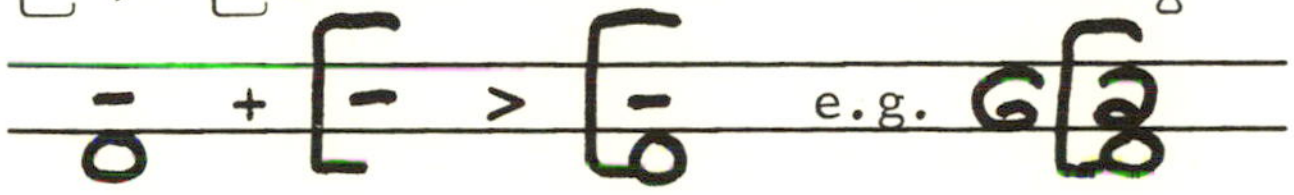

typed ခြွေ /hcwei/

ှ + ျ ; ျ is shortened:

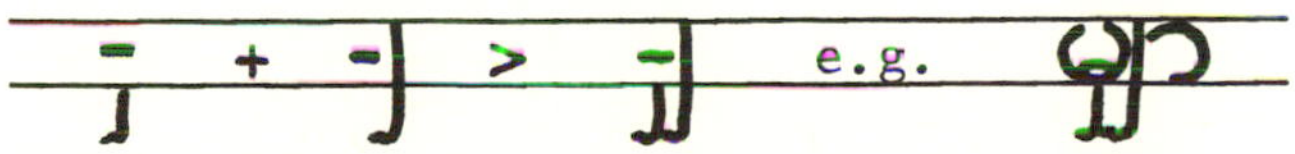

typed မျှာ /hmya/

ှ + ြ ; ှ is written inside ြ :

typed မြှော /hmyo:/

ွ + ှ + ြ (rare):

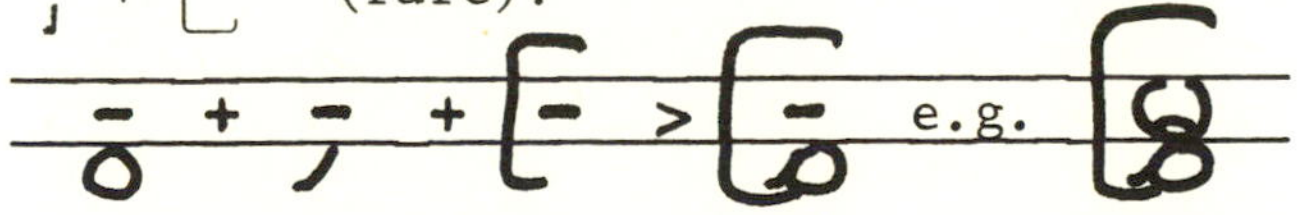

typed မြွှ (irregular pronunciation)

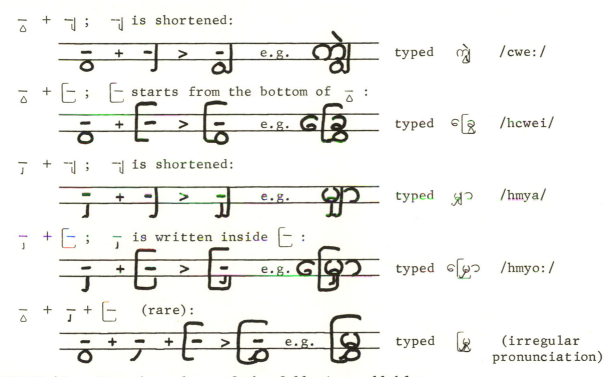

QUESTION 40: Give the values of the following syllables.

ကျွဲ ______	နွှေ ______	မျှာ ______
/cwe:/	/hnwei/	/hmya/
ခြွေ ______	ယွှီ ______	လွှ ______
/hcwei/	/hywi/	/hlwa./

မွှာ ______________	ကြွ ______________	မျှော ______________
/hmwa/	/cwa./	/hmyo:/
လွှဲ ______________	ညှော ______________	ရွှေ ______________
/hlwe:/	/hnyo:/	/hywei/

SUMMARY:

There are four medial consonant symbols in Burmese, representing three sounds. These symbols and the initials with which they occur are:

/-y/:

ျ /ya. pin./ occurs with:

ပ , ဖ , ဗ , ဘ , မ , က , ခ , ဂ

ြ /ya. yi'/ occurs with:

ပ , ဖ , ဗ , ဘ , မ , က , ခ , ဂ , င

/-w/: ွ /wa. hswe:/ occurs with all consonant symbols <u>except</u>:

ဃ , ဈ , ဋ , ဌ , ဍ , ဎ , ဏ , ဝ , ဠ

/h-/: ှ /ha. htou:/ occurs with:

င , ည , ဏ , န , မ , ယ , ရ , လ , ဝ

Now go on to Review Test 2.

REVIEW TEST 2.

SECTION A: Give the values of the following syllables.

1.	ကွာ ____________	2.	ညု ____________	3.	ဍော ____________
4.	နှိ ____________	5.	မျူ ____________	6.	ဓွာ ____________
7.	ရို ____________	8.	ဟာ ____________	9.	ချိ ____________
10.	ဆွဲ ____________	11.	ကျူ ____________	12.	ပွာ ____________
13.	ဗြိ ____________	14.	လျော ____________	15.	ငြို ____________
16.	ဋာ ____________	17.	နှွဲ ____________	18.	ဖြော ____________
19.	ယျူ ____________	20.	ဋါ ____________	21.	ဂျိ ____________
22.	သွဲ ____________	23.	စာ ____________	24.	မို ____________
25.	ပြေ ____________	26.	ရှိ ____________	27.	မွ ____________
28.	သော ____________	29.	နွေ ____________	30.	ညြို ____________
31.	တွာ ____________	32.	ဝိ ____________	33.	ကျော ____________
34.	ဘွာ ____________	35.	အိ ____________	36.	ကြွဲ ____________
37.	ချို ____________	38.	နွာ ____________	39.	ဋါ ____________
40.	ငေါ ____________	41.	လွ ____________	42.	တို ____________
43.	စွေ ____________	44.	ကိ ____________	45.	ခါ ____________
46.	ယွဲ ____________	47.	ဃ ____________	48.	ဒွေ ____________
49.	ဂေါ ____________	50.	ဖွိ ____________	51.	ရွှေ ____________

SECTION B: Write the following syllables in Burmese.

1. /hko:/ _____   2. /hpou/ _____

3. /hswe:/ _____   4. /pyei/ _____

5. /qa./   _____   6. /ci./   _____

7. /su/   _____   8. /byou/ _____

9. /hmo:/ _____   10. /nu./ _____

11. /hyei/ _____   12. /wa/   _____

13. /hkwe:/ _____   14. /nyu/ _____

15. /hou/ _____   16. /thwa/ _____

17. /hlu./ _____   18. /do:/ _____

19. /hnga/ _____   20. /hcu/ _____

21. /hmyei/ _____   22. /hti/ _____

23. /cwa./ _____   24. /zu/   _____

25. /hnou/ _____   26. /hyi./ _____

27. /hmwa/ _____ 28. /go:/ _____

29. /pyu./ _____ 30. /hsi/ _____

31. /bwe:/ _____ 32. /ta/ _____

33. /ngu./ _____ 34. /nyi./ _____

35. /hpya./ _____ 36. /htwei/ _____

37. /hcu./ _____ 38. /za/ _____

39. /hmyo:/ _____ 40. /hnyo:/ _____

41. /thi./ _____ 42. /hywe:/ _____

43. /qu/ _____ 44. /ga/ _____

45. /sa./ _____ 46. /di/ _____

47. /hlwe:/ _____ 48. /wei/ _____

49. /cou/ _____ 50. /ywa/ _____

REVIEW TEST 2: ANSWERS.

SECTION A:

1.	/kwa/	2.	/nyu./	3.	/do:/
4.	/hni/	5.	/myu/	6.	/zwa/
7.	/you/	8.	/ha/	9.	/hci/
10.	/hswe:/	11.	/htu/	12.	/pwa/
13.	/byi/	14.	/hlo:/	15.	/nyou/
16.	/ta/	17.	/hnwe:/	18.	/hpyo:/
19.	/hyu/	20.	/lu./	21.	/ji./
22.	/thwe:/	23.	/sa/	24.	/dou/
25.	/pyei/	26.	/hyi./	27.	/mwa./
28.	/tho:/	29.	/hcwei/	30.	/hnyou/
31.	/twa/	32.	/wi./	33.	/co:/
34.	/bwa/	35.	/qi/	36.	/cwe:/
37.	/zou/	38.	/nwa/	39.	/htu/
40.	/hngo:/	41.	/lwa./	42.	/tou/
43.	/swei/	44.	/ni/	45.	/hka/
46.	/ywe:/	47.	/ga./	48.	/dwei/
49.	/go:/	50.	/hpwi./	51.	/hywei/

SECTION B:

1.	ခေါ	2.	ဖို
3.	ဆွဲ	4.	ပျေ ပြေ
5.	အ	6.	ကျို ကြို
7.	ရှု	8.	ချို ဘျို ခြို ဘြို
9.	မှော	10.	နို
11.	ယှော ရှော	12.	ဓိ
13.	ခွဲ	14.	ညှု

15. ပ္ပ္   16. သွာ

17. ဈ   18. ဒေါ်   ဈော

19. ဂ္ဂ   20. ချ   ြဂ

21. ဈွေ   ြမ္ဈ   22. ဆ္ဆ

23. ကွ   ြဆ္ဆ   24. ရ္ဂ   ရှ

25. ဆ္ဈ   26. ထ္ထ   ရှ

27. ဈွာ   28. ဂေါ်

29. ြု   ြပ   30. ဆ္ဆ

31. ဒ္ဒ   ဒ္ဒ   32. တာ

33. ရ   34. ြည

35. ြ   ြဖ   36. ထွေ

37. ချ   ြဂ   38. ဇာ   ရာ

39. ြေ   ြမ္ဈာ   40. ဈ္ဈော

41. သ္ဆ   42. ထွဲ   ဒွဲ

43. အ္ရ   44. ဂါ

45. ဝ   46. ဒ္ဒ   ဈ္ဆ

47. ထွဲ   48. ဝေ

49. က္ရ္ဂ   ြက္ရ   50. ယွာ   ရှာ

CHAPTER 3

TONES

You have learned that each vowel symbol represents a tone as well as a vowel quality; we will call this the basic tone of the symbol. Many non-basic tones are represented with separate tone signs.

You know that ○ /i./, ┬ /u./, and [zero] /a./ represent vowels with tone III, and that each adds a single line to form the tone I vowel symbols ○ /i/, ┬ /u/, and ─ ၁ /a/. Tone II is formed by adding a new symbol to the tone I vowels:

Symbol	Transcription	Burmese Name	Translation
─:	/:/ (Tone II)	/hyei.ga. pau'/	dots ahead

This is written to the right of all other elements in a syllable, as, for example:

မိ: /mi:/

လာ: /la:/   ပါ: /pa:/

ကူ: /ku:/   [ဖြူ]: /hpyu:/

With these vowels, then, there is a tone progression:

	Tone III (basic)		Tone I		Tone II
/i/	○	add one stroke	○	further add :	○:
/u/	┬		┬		┬:
/a/	[zero]		─ ၁		─ ၁:

QUESTION 41: Give the values of the following syllables.

ဘူ: _____   ခါ: _____   ညီ: _____

/bu:/   /hka:/   /nyi:/

တော _____   သူ _____   လှူး _____
        /to:/   /thu/   /hlu:/

ကျ _____   သွား: _____   လဲ _____
        /ca./   /thwa:/   /le:/

ပြူး: _____   မှိ: _____   ရာ: _____
        /hpyu:/   /hmi:/   /ya:/

QUESTION 42: Write the following syllables in Burmese.

/ka:/ _____   /myi:/ _____

                ကား:   မှိ:   မြီ:

/hsu./ _____   /po:/ _____

                ဆု   ပေါ

/nyi./ _____   /nga:/ _____

                ညှ   ငါ:

/si:/ _____   /hyu:/ _____

                စီ:   ရှူး:   ရှူး:

/the:/ _____   /hcu:/ _____

                သဲ   ချူး:   ချုး:

The symbols ေ— and ◌ု represent vowels in tone I. To change them to tone II, add —: /hyei.ga. pau'/ at the end of the syllable as above. For example:

ေလ: /lei:/   ေဆွ: /hswei:/   ကို: /kou:/   ချို: /hcou:/

To change these vowels to tone III, a different symbol is used:

Symbol	Transcription	Burmese Name	Translation
—:	/./ (Tone III)	/qau'ka. myi'/ (or /qau'myi'/)	stopped below

For example:

        ေမ့ /mei./   ေလ့ /lei./   တို့ /tou./   မှို့ /hmou./

⸱ /qau'ka. myi'/ is generally written below and just to the right of a syllable, as above. Sometimes, however, particularly when the lower right-hand
corner of a syllable is crowded with other symbols, ⸱ /qau'ka. myi'/ occurs
further to the left:

           ကြို beside ကြို့ /cou./

           ေကြ beside ေကြ့ /cei./

With these vowels, then, the tone progression is:

	Tone I (basic)		Tone II		Tone III
/ei/	ေ—	add ꞉	ေ—꞉	or add ⸱	ေ—⸱
/ou/	◌ို		◌ို꞉		◌ို⸱

QUESTION 43: Give the values of the following syllables.

နို့ _____	ေတွ့ _____	ညို꞉ _____
/nou./	/twei./	/nyou:/

ဇိ꞉ _____	ဘို့ _____	ေပ꞉ _____
/zi:/	/bou./	/pei:/

ေဟ့ _____	ေသွ꞉ _____	ဖာ꞉ _____
/hei./	/thwei:/	/hpa:/

ဌ _____	ကြို꞉ _____	လဲ _____
/hta./	/cou:/	/hle:/

QUESTION 44: Write the following syllables in Burmese.

/lou./ _____   /htei:/ _____

         လို့   ေထ꞉

/byou./ _____   /hyei./ _____

ဗြို့. ဘြို့. ပြို့. ဖြို့.   ေလွ့.   ေရှ.

/hko:/ _____   /hmou:/ _____

ခေါ်   မှို:

/hkwei:/ _____   /hsou:/ _____

ခွေး:   ဆို:

/wei/ _____   /cwei./ _____

ေဝ   ေကျွ.   ေကြွ.

The symbols ေ —ာ and ◌ၱ represent vowels in tone II. To change them to
tone III, add ◌ৢ /qau'ka. myi'/ as above. For example:

ေတာ့ /to./   ေပါ့ /po./   မဲ့ /me./   ယဲ့ /ye./

To change ေ —ာ to tone I, a new symbol is added:

Symbol   Transcription   Burmese Name   Translation

◌ၱ   /-/ (Tone I)   /hyei. htou:/   thrust forward

It is written: 𝗖   with —ာ or —ါ , as in:

ေမာ် /mo/   ေတာ် /to/   ေပါ် /po/   ေခါ် /hko/

For the vowel /e/ in tone I, ◌ၱ /nau' pyi'/ is dropped entirely. Instead,
the initial consonant is followed by ဝ /ya. pale'/ plus the symbol ◌ၱ , written as with ေ —ာ , i.e.:

ဝ + 𝗖 > ဝ𝗖

as in:

ဆ ယ် /hse/   ခွ ယ် /hkwe/   ကျ ယ် /ce/

The name /hyei. htou:/, however, is used only when ◌ၱ occurs with ေ —ာ ;
elsewhere ◌ၱ occurs with consonants and is known as /qatha'/ "killer," since

it "kills" the /a./ that follows an unmarked consonant. For example, the
sequence ဝယ is read /wa. ya./, but ဝယ်, with /qatha'/, is read /we/. The
/a./ of ယ /ya./ has been "killed," and ယ် /ya. pale'/ with /qatha'/ represents /e/, forming one syllable with the preceding ဝ /w/.

When /qatha'/ is spelled in combination with a consonant, the /qa=/
prefix is dropped, and /tha'/ follows the name of the consonant:

Symbol	Transcription	Burmese Name	Translation
– ယ်	/e/	/ya. tha'/ (or /ya. pale' tha'/)	killed <u>ya</u> (or killed supine <u>ya</u>)[1]

QUESTION 45: Now give the values of the following syllables.

ခေါ် _____	ကြယ် _____	မာ _____
/hko/	/ce/	/ma/

အဲ့ _____	ဒိ _____	ပေါ့ _____
/qe./	/di./	/po./

နေ့ _____	ဘယ် _____	ယယ် _____
/nei./	/be/	/ye/

စဲ့ _____	ဝဲ _____	ဖျော် _____
/se./	/we:/	/hpyo/

QUESTION 46: Write the following syllables in Burmese.

/he./ _____	/tho:/ _____
ဟဲ့	သော

/ne/ _____	/ngo./ _____
နယ်	ငေါ့

---

1. Since ရ /ya.gau'/ only rarely occurs with ် /qatha'/, the term /ya.
    tha'/ regularly refers to ယ် /ya. pale' tha'/. The longer name is used
    only for direct contrast with /ya.gau' tha'/.

/co/ _____   /yu./ _____

ကျော် ‌ကြော်   ယု ရု

/hso./ _____   /le/ _____

‌ဆော့   လယ်

/pyo/ _____   /ho/ _____

‌ပျော် ‌ပြော်   ‌ဟော်

/pwe:/ _____   /cwe/ _____

ပွဲ   ကျွယ် ‌ကြွယ်

SUMMARY:

The following chart shows the writing of each vowel in tones I, II, and III.

	Tone I	Tone II	Tone III
/a/	— ာ (−ါ)	— ား (−ါး)	[0]
/i/	ိ	ိး	ီ
/u/	ု (−ု)	ူး (−ူး)	ူ (−ူ)
/ei/	‌ေ−	‌ေ−း	‌ေ−့
/e/	−ယ်	ဲ	ဲ့
/o/	‌ေ−ာ် (‌ေ−ႆ)	‌ေ−ာ (‌ေ−ါ)	‌ေ−ာ့ (‌ေ−ါ့)
/ou/	ုိ (−ုိ)	ုိး (−ုိး)	ုိ့ (−ုိ့)

If we set up a vowel triangle as follows:[2]

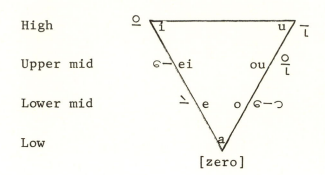

High

Upper mid

Lower mid

Low

[zero]

Then:

The three corners (high and low vowels):   /i/   /u/   /a/

    Tone III - basic

    Tone I - add one stroke

    Tone II - further add ─: /hyei.ga. pau'/

Upper mid vowels: /ei/   /ou/

    Tone I - basic

    Tone II - add ─: /hyei.ga. pau'/

    Tone III - add ╌ /qau'ka. myi'/

Lower mid vowels: /e/   /o/

    Tone II - basic

    Tone III - add ╌ /qau'ka. myi'/

    Tone I - involves ⌒ (/qatha'/ with ─ω ;
                     /hyei. htou:/ with ⌐─ᴐ)

───
2. I am indebted to Mr. John Okell of the School of Oriental and African
    Studies, University of London, for suggesting this simple method of
    summary to me and for his kind permission to use it here.

Or, in another form (with basic tone symbols underlined):

	Tone III	Tone I	Tone II
/i, u, a/	(symbols) [0]	(symbols)	(symbols)
/ei, ou/	(symbols)	(symbols)	(symbols)
/e, o/	(symbols)	(symbols)	(symbols)

Now go on to Review Test 3 on tones I, II, and III. In the next
chapter we will take up the special problems of writing tone IV.

REVIEW TEST 3.

SECTION A: Give the values of the following syllables.

1. ဂါး _____   2. ရျော် _____   3. ထယ် _____

4. ဖေး _____   5. ဖွဲ _____   6. ဒ _____

7. ဒေါ့ _____   8. ရ _____   9. ဗို့း _____

10. ဂြားး _____   11. ဟော _____   12. နွဲ _____

13. တု _____   14. မြို _____   15. အော့ _____

16. ချယ် _____   17. ဂျူ _____   18. မိး _____

19. ဟို့း _____   20. ညော _____   21. ရဲ _____

22. ကြူး _____   23. ဒီ _____   24. သွားး _____

25. နေးး _____   26. ငဲ့ _____   27. လို့ _____

28. ဝိ _____   29. ပေ _____   30. ခြိုး _____

31. ညာ _____   32. တွဲ _____   33. မြို _____

34. ခေါ် _____   35. ယို _____   36. ရွဲး _____

37. ရျုး _____   38. ဇ _____   39. မဲ့ _____

40. ကျော့ _____   41. ဆိးး _____   42. နဲ့ _____

43. ဂျုး _____   44. ဗို့ _____   45. ပဲ့ _____

46. သေ၁ _____   47. ဝယ် _____   48. အိးး _____

SECTION B: Write the following syllables in Burmese.

1. /nyou:/ _____   2. /cei./ _____

3. /hko:/ _____   4. /ti./ _____

5. /hya:/ _____   6. /pe/ _____

7. /hsei:/ _____   8. /myou./ _____

9. /thi/ _____   10. /hko/ _____

11. /hmyu/ _____   12. /gu./ _____

13. /hmya./ _____   14. /so:/ _____

15. /di./ _____   16. /hmwei/ _____

17. /nou/ _____   18. /cwe:/ _____

19. /zu:/ _____   20. /hlwa/ _____

21. /bi/ _____   22. /ho./ _____

23. /nge/ _____   24. /to/ _____

25. /kou/ _____   26. /pyu./ _____

27. /wa:/ _____   28. /ne./ _____

29. /hcwei:/_____   30. /pyi:/ _____

REVIEW TEST 3:   ANSWERS.

SECTION A:

1.	/ga:/	2.	/zo/	3.	/hte/
4.	/hpei:/	5.	/hlwe:/	6.	/la./
7.	/do./	8.	/su./	9.	/bou:/
10.	/hya:/	11.	/ho:/	12.	/ngwei/
13.	/tu/	14.	/myou./	15.	/qo./
16.	/hcwe/	17.	/zu/	18.	/mi:/
19.	/hou:/	20.	/hnyo:/	21.	/ye./
22.	/cu:/	23.	/di/	24.	/thwa:/
25.	/hnei:/	26.	/nge./	27.	/lou./
28.	/wi./	29.	/pei./	30.	/hcou:/
31.	/nya/	32.	/twe:/	33.	/nyi/
34.	/hko/	35.	/you/	36.	/swei:/
37.	/zu:/	38.	/da./	39.	/me./
40.	/co./	41.	/hsi:/	42.	/htei:/
43.	/bu:/	44.	/hpou./	45.	/wei:/
46.	/tho/	47.	/ye/	48.	/qi:/

SECTION B:

1. လိုး:   2. ကျေ   ကြေ

3. ခေါ   4. တိ

5. ဃာ:   ၇ာ:   6. ပယ်

7. ဆေ:   8. ရှို   ပြို

9. သို   10. ခေါ

11. ရှဲ   ပြဲ   12. ၇

13. ရှဲ   ပြ   14. ေလာ

15. ဒိ   ၀ိ   16. ေပြ

17. နို့

18. ကျဲ   ကြဲ

19. ရး   ျူး

20. လွာ

21. ဖိ   အိ

22. ဟော့

23. ငယ်

24. တော်

25. ကို့

26. ျာ   ပြါ

27. ဝါး

28. နဲ့

29. ချေး   ရွေး

30. ပို း   ပြီး

CHAPTER 4

CLOSED SYLLABLES

So far you have learned syllables which end with a vowel or with a symbol for tone I, II, or III; these are known as "open" syllables. But elsewhere you have also seen syllables in the transcription which end with /'/
(tone IV) or /-n/ (nasalization); these are "closed" syllables and are usually
written in Burmese with a final consonant. Such consonants, like ဝ် in the
preceding chapter, are regularly marked with ◌် /qatha'/ "killer" to show
that they do not begin a new syllable.

Many closed syllables consist only of an initial and a final consonant;
in such cases the final consonant represents not only tone IV or final /-n/,
but a vowel quality as well. For example, the vowel /a/ in closed syllables
is written with one of the following symbols, all without separate vowel symbol:

Tone IV: /-a'/   −တ် /ta. tha'/

                          − ပ် /pa. tha'/

Final Nasal: /-an/   − န် /na. tha'/

                          − မ် /ma. tha'/

                           ◌ံ   /thei:dhei: tin/

The last of these is a new symbol, the name of which means "little thing put
on." It is written above the initial consonant in the same position as
/loun:ji: tin/.

Here are some syllables with these finals:

    ပတ် /pa'/   ခပ် /hka'/

    ကန် /kan/   ကံ /can/   လန်: /lan:/

Notice the last example. For ALL regular syllables ending with a final nasal,
such as − န် , − မ် , or ◌ံ , tone I is basic, tone II is written with −:
/hyei.ga. pau'/, and tone III is written with ◌့ /qau'ka. myi'/. For example:

62

Tone I: လန် /lan/   ဆံ /hsan/

Tone II: လန်း /lan:/   ဆံး /hsan:/

Tone III: လန့် /lan./   ဆံ့ /hsan./

QUESTION 47: Give the values of the following syllables.

မှံ့ _____   လစ် _____   အံး: _____
      /hman/   /la'/   /qan:/

ခါး: _____   တတ် _____   နန့် _____
      /hka:/   /ta'/   /nan./

ဆန်: _____   ဖတ် _____   ပြံ့ _____
      /hsan:/   /hpa'/   /pyan./

သစ် _____   ငံ့ _____   စန် _____
      /tha'/   /ngan./   /san/

QUESTION 48: Write the following syllables in Burmese.

/hkan/ _____   /sa'/ _____

           ခန် ခံ ခံ့   စတ်   စစ်

/ca'/ _____   /ca./ _____

      ကျတ် ကျစ် ကြတ် ကြစ်   ကျ   ကြ

/htan:/ _____   /qan./ _____

           ထန်: ထံ: ထံ:   အန့် အံ့ အံ့

/hya'/ _____   /hman:/ _____

      ယှတ် ယှစ် ရှတ် ရှစ်   မှန်: မှံ: မှံ:

/ha/ _____   /nyan/ _____

              ဟာ   ညန် ညံ ညံ

/hnan./ _____   /hpan:/ _____

ﾖ§ﾒ ﾖ♀ﾒ ﾒﾒ·   ０§: ０♀: ·:

This set of final consonants also occurs with certain of the vowel symbols, but the latter have different values in such closed syllables from
those you have learned for them in open syllables. For example, ̥ /loun:ji:
tin/ with these finals represents the vowel quality /ei/ (not /i/):

       Tone IV: /-ei'/   ̥ﾒ /loun:ji: tin, ta. tha'/

                         ̥ ﾒ /loun:ji: tin, pa. tha'/

       Final Nasal: /-ein/   ̥ § /loun:ji: tin, na. tha'/

                         ̥ ♀ /loun:ji: tin, ma. tha'/

Note, however, that ̈ /thei:dhei: tin/ and ̥ /loun:ji: tin/, which occupy
the same space over the initial consonant, almost never occur together in a
syllable. Do not write this combination in the exercises.

   Examples of closed syllables with /ei/ are:

    သိတ် /thei'/   စိန် /sein/   မိန်: /mein:/

    လိဒ် /lei'/   အိမ် /qein/   နိ♀ /nein./

Again, you can see that the nasal final is basically tone I, adding ̄:
/hyei.ga. pau'/ for tone II, or ̣ /qau'ka. myi'/ for tone III.

QUESTION 49: Give the values of the following syllables.

ပိတ် _____   ဒိ♀ _____   ဆေ: _____
        /pei'/   /dein./   /hsei:/

မိတ် _____   စိ _____   ခ္ျိန် _____
        /mei'/   /si./   /hcein/

နိ် _____   ဟေ· _____   ညိမ် _____
        /hnei'/   /hei./   /nyein/

တိန်: _____   အိ§ﾒ _____   ယိမ်: _____
        /tein:/   /qein./   /yein:/

QUESTION 50: Write the following syllables in Burmese.

/hsei'/ _____   /zei:/ _____

         ဆိတ်   ဆိပ်   ေဇး   ေဇျး

/kan/ _____   /mein./ _____

         ကန်   ကမ်   ကံ   မိန့်   မိန့်

/thei'/ _____   /bein:/ _____

         သိတ်   သိပ်   ဗိန်း ဗိမ်း   ဘိန်း ဘိမ်း

/thi./ _____   /hta'/ _____

              သိ   ထတ်   ထပ်

/hnein/ _____   /cei'/ _____

         နှိန်   နှိမ်   ကျိတ် ကျိပ် ကြိတ် ကြိပ်

These final consonants also occur with ◌ု /tahcaun: ngin/, which has the
value /ou/ (not /u/) in closed syllables:

> Tone IV: /-ou'/   ◌ုတ် /tahcaun: ngin, ta. tha'/
>
>   ◌ုပ် /tahcaun: ngin, pa. tha'/
>
> Final Nasal: /-oun/   ◌ုန် /tahcaun: ngin, na. tha'/
>
>   ◌ုမ် /tahcaun: ngin, ma. tha'/
>
>   ◌ုံ /tahcaun: ngin, thei:dhei: tin/

as in:

> ဟုတ် /hou'/   လုပ် /lou'/   ချုပ် /hcou'/
>
> ကုန် /koun/   သုန်: /thoun:/   လှုမ် /hloun/   ရှုံ. /hyoun./

The combination ◌ုမ် , however, is rare, and you need not write it in the
exercises; in general, /-oun/ is written either ◌ုန် or ◌ုံ . The conditions
for using the long and short forms of /tahcaun: ngin/ are the same in closed
syllables as in open ones.

QUESTION 51: Give the values of the following syllables.

လု _____   မုန်ႆ _____   လိုꩦ _____
         /hu./   /moun./   /lou/

ရှိုꩦႊ _____   ပြုန်ႆ _____   နိုꩦ. _____
        /hyoun:/   /byoun/   /nou./

စိုꩦ. _____   လှုဝ် _____   သုန်ႊ _____
        /soun./   /hlou'/   /thoun:/

ကျိုဝ် _____   ဖုꩦ _____   ညှုတ် _____
        /cou'/   /hpoun/   /hnyou'/

QUESTION 52: Write the following syllables in Burmese.

/hsou:/ _____   /hkou'/ _____

             ဆိုꩦႊ   ခုတ်   ခုဝ်

/pyu./ _____   /qoun:/ _____

             ပျု   ြပ   အုန်ႊ   အိုꩦႊ

/hmou'/ _____   /tou./ _____

             မှုတ်   မှုဝ်   တိုꩦ.

/hmyou'/ _____   /koun/ _____

      မျှတ် မျှဝ် ြမှတ် ြမှဝ်   ကုန်   ကိုꩦ

/lu:/ _____   /ngoun./ _____

             လူꩦႊ   ငုန်ႆ   ငိုꩦ.

Finally, these five final consonants also occur in syllables with the
vowel /u/. This vowel, however, is represented neither with a vowel symbol
nor as inherent in a final consonant, but with written w. The combination
/wu-/ is represented with initial ဝ /wa./, as in:

Tone IV: /wu'/   ○တ်   /wa., ta. tha'/

                             ○ပ်   /wa., pa. tha'/

Final Nasal: /wun/   ○န်   /wa., na. tha'/

                             ○မ်   /wa., ma. tha'/

                             ○̇   /wa., thei:dhei: tin/

With any other initial consonant, /u/ is represented with ◌ /wa. hswe:/:

Tone IV: /-u'/   ◌တ်   /wa. hswe:, ta. tha'/

                             ◌ပ်   /wa. hswe:, pa. tha'/

Final Nasal: /-un/   ◌န်   /wa. hswe:, na. tha'/

                             ◌မ်   /wa. hswe:, ma. tha'/

                             ◌̇   /wa. hswe:, thei:dhei: tin/

Examples of syllables with these last combinations are:

   ချုတ်   /hcu'/   ဈုပ်   /su'/

   ကွန်   /kun/   ဆွမ်: /hsun:/   ကျွ.   /cun./

QUESTION 53: Give the values of the following syllables.

ကျွန် _____   လွုတ် _____   ပြု _____

/cun/   /lu'/   /pyu./

ပြုတ် _____   ○̇ _____   ချုဝ် _____

/pyou'/   /wun/   /hcu'/

ထွမ်: _____   ○န့် _____   ဆွဲ _____

/htun:/   /wun./   /hswe:/

○မ်: _____   ○ပ် _____   စွ̇ _____

/wun:/   /wu'/   /sun/

ညွန်: _____   ည̇. _____   ○တ် _____

/hnyun:/   /hyun./   /wu'/

QUESTION 54:   Write the following syllables in Burmese.

/wun/   _____   /du./   _____

ဝန်   ဝမ်   ဝံ   ဒု   ဓု

/htu:/   _____   /lou'/   _____

ထူး   လုတ်   လုပ်

/hmun:/ _____   /hcu'/   _____

မှုန်း   မှုမ်း   မှုံး   ချုတ်   ချုပ်   ခြုတ်   ခြုပ်

/hkwei:/ _____   /hsun./ _____

ခွေး   ဆွန့်   ဆွမ့်   ဆွုံ့.

/wu'/   _____   /hlu'/   _____

ဝတ်   ဝပ်   လှုတ်   လှုပ်

So far we have considered the finals — တ် , — ပ် , — န် , — မ် , and — ံ ,
but three other consonants occur commonly in final position. Like the first
five, they sometimes appear in syllables without vowel symbol, in which case
they represent a vowel quality as well as /'/ or /-n/.

— က် /ka. tha'/ in such syllables represents the vowel /e/:

        Tone IV: /-e'/   — က် /ka. tha'/

There is no corresponding nasal syllable with /-en/ in Burmese. Examples of
syllables with /-e'/ are:

        တက် /te'/   မျက် /pye'/   ငှက် /hnge'/

QUESTION 55: Give the values of the following syllables.

မျက် _____   လယ် _____   လက် _____
        /mye'/   /le/   /le'/

ခက် _____   နဲ့. _____   ကြက် _____
        /hke'/   /ne./   /ce'/

ဆတ် _____   ဝတ် _____   ငှက် _____
/hsa'/   /wu'/   /hnge'/

The last two common finals are − ⑥ and − ⑤ . These represent vowel /i/ when no vowel symbol is present:

Tone IV: /-i'/   − ⑥   /sa. tha'/

Final Nasal: /-in/   − ⑤   /nga. tha'/

as in:

တစ် /ti'/   မြစ် /myi'/

ဆင် /hsin/   ကင်း /kin:/   ဖြင့် /hpyin./

QUESTION 56: Give the values of the following syllables.

ရှင် _____   မြင့် _____   ဆင်း _____
/hyin/   /myin./   /hsin:/

နီး _____   လံ့ _____   ကျစ် _____
/ni:/   /lan./   /ci'/

ချိန် _____   ပစ် _____   ကင်း _____
/hcein/   /pyi'/   /kin:/

QUESTION 57: Write the following syllables in Burmese.

/si'/ _____   /yin/ _____
               စစ်   ဝင်   ရင်

/ti./ _____   /hsin./ _____
               တိ   ဆင့်

/thei'/ _____   /hmin/ _____
            သိတ်   သိပ်   မှင်

/hpyin./ _____   /lein:/ _____
            ဖျင့်   ဖြင့်   လိန်း   လိမ်း

/nyi'/ _____   /ngin:/ _____

ည် /sa. tha'/ does not normally occur in syllables with vowel symbols.
But —က် /ka. tha'/ and —င် /nga. tha'/ occur with the combinations ေ—ာ
and ိ . Once again, the vowel symbols have different values from those they
had in open syllables: ေ—ာ represents /au/ (not /o:/), ိ represents /ai/
(not /ou/):

        Tone IV: /-au'/ ေ—ာက် /thawei htou:, yei: hca., ka. tha'/

                      /-ai'/   ိက် /loun:ji: tin, tahcaun: ngin, ka. tha'/

        Final Nasal: /-aun/ ေ—ာင် /thawei htou:, yei: hca., nga. tha'/

                      /-ain/   ိင် /loun:ji: tin, tahcaun: ngin, nga. tha'/

Examples are:

    အောက် /qau'/   ပေါက် /pau'/   တိုက် /tai'/   ပြိုက် /pyai'/

    မောင် /maun/   ခေါင်: /hkaun:/   ဆိုင် /hsain/   ကျိုင့် /cain./

The long variants —ါ , and —ုု are used in the same way as in open syllables.
QUESTION 58: Give the values of the following syllables.

    မိုက် _____   ကိုင်: _____   လောက် _____
          /mai'/   /kain:/   /lau'/

    အောင် _____   ဘို _____   ဟုတ် _____
          /qaun/   /bou/   /hou'/

    ခေါ _____   ထောက် _____   ကျိုင့် _____
        /hko:/   /htau'/   /jain./

    နိုင် _____   စိုက် _____   ဆောင်: _____
        /nain/   /sai'/   /hsaun:/

QUESTION 59: Write the following syllables in Burmese.

    /tain./ _____   /kaun:/ _____

            တိုင့်   ကောင်:

/ngau'/ _____ ဝေါ်က်

/yain:/ _____ ယှိုင်း ရှိုင်း

/hcai'/ _____ ချို့က် ခြို့က်

/pyo:/ _____ ပျော် ခ[ပှာ

/paun/ _____ ပေါင်

/dou:/ _____ ဒို့း ရို့း

/qain/ _____ အိုင်

/hnau'/ _____ နှောက်

Finally, –က် /ka. tha'/ and –င် /nga. tha'/ also occur in syllables with ဝ /wa./ and ◌ွ /wa. hswe:/. In these forms, however, the vowel is represented by the final consonant or a vowel symbol; ဝ and ◌ွ represent only /w/, as they do in open syllables. For example:

ဝက် /we'/ ထွက် /htwe'/

ဝင် /win/ ဖွင့် /hpwin./ ဝိုင် /wain/

QUESTION 60: Give the values of these syllables with ဝ and ◌ွ .

ခွတ် _____ /hku'/ ခွက် _____ /hkwe'/ ခွဲ _____ /hkwe:/

ဆွမ်း _____ /sun:/ ကွင် _____ /kwin/ ဖွင့် _____ /hpwin./

ညွှန့် _____ /nyun./ ကြွ _____ /cun/ ဝက် _____ /we'/

ဝတ် _____ /wu'/ ဒွိ _____ /du'/ ဝင်း _____ /win:/

SUMMARY:

In most closed syllables without vowel symbol, the final consonant represents a vowel as well as /'/ (tone IV) or /-n/ (nasalization):

    −ဎ် /-e'/

    −ဒ် /-i'/   − င် /-in/

    −ဎ် }
    − ဒ် } /-a'/   − ၌ }
                    − ဒ် } /-an/
                      ़ }

But symbols ဝ /wa./ and ${}_{\triangle}^{-}$ /wa. hswe:/ represent /u/ with −ဎ် , − ဒ် , − ၌ , − ဒ် , and ़ ; they represent only initial or medial /w/ with −ဎ် and − င် .

Four vowel symbols occur in closed syllables, where they have different values from those they represent in open syllables:

    ${}^{\circ}_{-}$C /ei/ (open syllable: /i./)

    ${}_{\iota}^{-}$C /ou/ (open syllable: /u./)

    ၆−ɔC /au/ (open syllable: /o:/)

    ${}^{\circ}_{\iota}$ C /ai/ (open syllable: /ou/)

If we put the vowels into a triangle again:

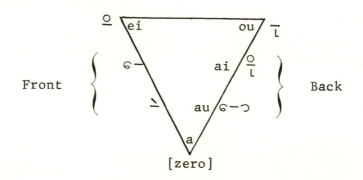

Then:

    The corners plus ဝ and ${}_{\triangle}^{-}$:

        occur with   −ဎ် , − ဒ် , − ၌ , − ဒ် , and ़

        EXCEPT: ${}^{\circ}_{-}$ almost never occurs with ़

        ${}_{\iota}^{-}$ is rare with − ဒ်

Back:

occur with —ိုက် and — င်

Front:

do not normally occur in closed syllables

Plus:

Zero occurs with: — စ် and — င် for /i/

— ိုက် for /e/

Closed syllables, then, are written with the following combinations:

	Tone IV (/-'/)	Final Nasal (/-n/)
/e/	—ိုက်	
/i/	— စ်	— င်
/au/	ေ—ာက်	ေ—ာင်
/ai/	ို̲က်	ို̲င်
/a/	—က် , — တ်	— န် , — မ် , —ံ
/ei/	ိုက် , ို တ်	ို န် , ို မ်
/ou/	ုိက် , ုိ တ်	ုိ န် ,(ုိ မ်), ုံ
/u/	ူက် , ူ တ်	ူ န် , ူ မ် , ူံ
[/wu-/	ဝက် , ဝတ်	ဝန် , ဝမ် , ဝံ]

Tone markings for syllables with final nasals (— င် , — န် , — မ် , —ံ)
are:

Tone I: unmarked (basic)

Tone II: —: /hyei.ga. pau'/

Tone III: —့ /qau'ka. myi'/

Now go on to Review Test 4, covering the entire set of closed syllables.
The test includes some open syllables too, to keep them fresh in your mind.

REVIEW TEST 4.

SECTION A: Give the values of the following syllables.

1. မြစ် _____   2. ဆွပ် _____   3. ပျက် _____

4. တိုက် _____   5. လို့. _____   6. ဟုတ် _____

7. ချိပ် _____   8. ၄က် _____   9. သွင် _____

10. ထီ _____   11. အောက် _____   12. နှမ်း _____

13. က _____   14. ရွှေ့ _____   15. ဝက် _____

16. ကြ: _____   17. ၉စ် _____   18. ဖျံ့ _____

19. လမ်း _____   20. သင့် _____   21. ယိန် _____

22. ထွက် _____   23. ကြဲ့ _____   24. စစ် _____

25. ခေါ် _____   26. မိုက် _____   27. ဝင်: _____

28. ဒေါင့် _____   29. အိတ် _____   30. လယ် _____

SECTION B: Write the following syllables in Burmese.

1. /mun/ _____   2. /sa'/ _____

3. /ti'/ _____   4. /pyei/ _____

5. /yei'/ _____   6. /loun:/ _____

7. /htau'/_____   8. /mou./ _____

9. /we/ _____   10. /hni'/ _____

11. /thi./ _____   12. /hku'/ _____

13. /kan:/ _____   14. /wain./ _____

15. /hya./ _____   16. /caun/ _____

17. /nyun./ _____   18. /hpei'/ _____

19. /we'/ _____   20. /twe:/ _____

21. /gu./ _____   22. /ngou'/ _____

23. /hmwa/ _____   24. /haun:/ _____

25. /hcin/ _____   26. /po/ _____

27. /hlou'/ _____   28. /bou/ _____

29. /dein:/ _____   30. /cu/ _____

REVIEW TEST 4:   ANSWERS.

SECTION A:

1. /myi'/	2. /hsu'/	3. /pya'/
4. /tai'/	5. /lou./	6. /hou'/
7. /hcei'/	8. /hnge'/	9. /thwin/
10. /hti/	11. /qau'/	12. /hnan:/
13. /ka./	14. /hywei/	15. /we'/
16. /can/	17. /hmou'/	18. /zun/
19. /lan:/	20. /thin./	21. /yein/
22. /htwe'/	23. /cwe:/	24. /si'/
25. /hko:/	26. /mai'/	27. /win:/
28. /daun./	29. /bei'/	30. /le/

SECTION B:

1. မွန် မွမ် မွဲ့   2. စတ် စပ်

3. တစ်   4. ပြေ ြပ

5. ယိတ် ယိပ် ရိတ် ရိပ်   6. လုန်း လုံး

7. ထောက်   8. မို့

9. ဝယ်   10. နှစ်

11. သိ   12. ခွတ် ခွပ်

13. ကန်း ကမ်း ကံး   14. ဗိုင့်

15. မှ ၇   16. ကျောင ကြောင

17. ညွန့် ညွမ့် ညွဲ့   18. ဖိတ် ဖိပ်

19. ဝက်   20. တွဲ

21. ၇   22. ၇တ် ၇ပ်

23. ၈ာ   24. ဟောင်း

25. ချင် ခြင်   26. ပေါ်

27. လှုတ် လှုပ်   28. ဗို ဘို

29. ၃င်: ၃ဉ်: ၈င်: ၈ဉ်:   30. ကျ။ ကြ။

One minor point has been omitted from the previous discussion of closed
syllables in order to avoid further complicating your learning of them. This
is the fact that − ဉ် /ma. tha'/ and ⁻̇ /thei:dhei: tin/ rarely occur in the
same type of syllable. You have already seen that normally − ဉ် occurs with
ㅇ̥ /loun:ji: tin/ while ⁻̇ does not, and that the reverse is true with ⁻ι
/tahcaun: ngin/. In syllables with vowel /a/ (no vowel symbol) or /u/ (⁻Δ
/wa. hswe:/ or ၀ /wa./) both finals appear, but − ဉ် is normally in syllables with tone II, ⁻̇ in those with tone I or tone III, that is:

သ̇ /hsan/	and	သ̥̇ /hsan./	but: သ ဉ်: /hsan:/
၃̇ /sun/		၃̥̇. /hsun./	၃ ဉ်: /hsun:/
၀̇ /wun/		၀̥̇ /wun./	၀ ဉ်: /wun:/

This distribution can be summarized as follows:

		Tone I	Tone II	Tone III
/-an/	[0]	⁻̇	− ဉ်:	⁻̇.
/-un/	⁻Δ			
/wun/	၀ −			
/-ein/	ㅇ̥	− ဉ်	− ဉ်:	− ဉ̥
/-oun/	⁻ι	⁻̇	⁻̇:	⁻̇.

(− ဉ̥ /na. tha'/ occurs in all these positions.)

CHAPTER 5

SYLLABLES IN SEQUENCE

So far you have learned to read and write only isolated syllables. In
this chapter we will consider some problems that occur with sequences of syllables.

Look at the following sentence and compare the Burmese writing with the
version in transcription:

အရင်ကစာတိုက်မှာ အလုပ်လုပ်တယ်

/qayin-ga. sa-dai'hma qalou' lou'te/

"Formerly (I) worked in the post office."

The first thing you will probably have noticed is that there are no
spaces separating words in the Burmese writing. At first this may give you
some difficulty in reading, butassoonasyouaresureoftheindividualwordsyouwill
havenodifficultyinknowinghowtodivideasentenceintoitspartscorrectly. Where
space occurs within a Burmese sentence, it normally marks a major break, such
as the end of a clause; even in such positions, however, there is often no
written space or punctuation.

Another problem that appears in the sentence above is the writing of
atonic syllables. These are the syllables we write in transcription with
the vowel /a/ immediately followed by another syllable, as in /qayin-ga./
"formerly," /qalou'/ "work," /ca-dhabadei:nei./ "Thursday," etc.

Atonic syllables are written in Burmese in the same way as those ending
in /a./, that is with a consonant or consonant cluster but no vowel symbol.
For example, the first syllables of /qayin-ga./ and /qalou'/ above are written အ , just as if you were writing the syllable /qa./. Compare this with
the last syllable of /qayin-ga./ where the lone consonant က does represent
a tone III syllable. (We'll discuss the shift from /ka./ to /ga./ in a
moment.) As you have seen in the transcription, atonic syllables occur only
initially or internally in a word, never finally, so that when you see a consonant without a vowel symbol at the end of a word it will regularly repre-

sent a syllable with /a./.

But when such consonants occur at the beginning of a word or internally, the writing is ambiguous. Compare, for example:

ကရင် /kayin/ "Karen" (a minority group of Burma)

ကရင် /ka.yin/ "if (he) dances"

or:

လမု /lamu./ (a kind of tree)

လမင်း /la.min:/ "moon"

In such situations you cannot derive the pronunciation of a word from any rules of spelling; you must simply know the word, just as in English you must know that bow "hunting implement" is pronounced differently from bow "front end of a boat."

QUESTION 61: In the following words and phrases, underline the syllables that could be atonic. The answers are also spelled out for you in transcription.

ခရီး	အဝတ်	ဗမာလို
ခရီး /hkayi:/	အဝတ် /qawu'/	ဗမာလို /bama-lou/
စနေနေ့	အင်မတန်	သောက်စရာ
စနေနေ့ /sanei-nei./	အင်မတန် /qin-matan/	သောက်စရာ /thau'saya/
ဆရာမ	ဘယ်သွားမလို့လဲ	ဘမှ
ဆရာမ /hsaya-ma./	ဘယ်သွားမလို့လဲ /be thwa:malou.le:/	None /ba-hma./

Again: remember that a word-final syllable is never atonic (first and third examples in the last line) and that there is no space between words in Burmese (middle example).

QUESTION 62:   Now try writing some words with atonic syllables in transcription.

ထမင်း   _____   အမျိုး   _____

         /htamin:/   /qamyou:/

မသွားဘူး _____   နှမ   _____

         /mathwa:bu:/   /hnama./

လုပ်သလား   _____   မီးရထား   _____

         /lou'thala:/   /mi:yahta:/

               ပဋမ   _____

                     /pahtama./

QUESTION 63:   Write the following words and phrases in Burmese.

/tahse/   _____   /qatwe'/   _____

             တဆယ်   အတွက်

/pawa/   _____   /mane'/   _____

             ပဝါ   မနက်

/thwa:mala:/   _____   /hsaun: qahka/ _____

             သွားမလား   ဆောင်းအခါ

/mani: mawei:/   _____   /hke'thala:/   _____

             မနိုးမဝေး   ခက်သလား

Syllable sequences further raise the problem of initial consonant voicing shifts within a word. You have learned that certain syllables have different initial consonants in different words. For example:

        /tha:/ "son," when it stands alone

    but: /-dha:/ in /yan-goun-dha:/ "native of Rangoon"

        /-te/ final particle, in /hou'te/ "is so"

    but: /-de/ in /thwa:de/ "goes"

/-hpu:/ negative particle, in /malou'hpu:/ "doesn't do"

      but: /-bu:/ in /maca.bu:/ "doesn't fall"

That is, consonants that are voiceless following pause or tone IV are re-
placed by their voiced counterparts after a syllable in tone I, II, or III.
The complete set of alternations is:

Initial or after tone IV		After tones I, II, III
hp, p	replaced by	b
ht, t		d
hs, s		z
hc, c		j
hk, k		g
th		dh

Such changes take place in the <u>pronunciation</u> of a given syllable, but
the <u>written</u> <u>form</u> remains unchanged. For example, consider the word အရင်က
/qayin-ga./ "formerly" in the sentence on page 78. The last syllable is the
noun particle /ka./ "from, source"; it is written က , and after a tone IV
syllable is pronounced with a /k/, as in အလုပ်က /qalou'ka./ "from work."
After the tone I syllable of /qayin/ "first, prior time," the pronunciation of the particle changes to /ga./, but the spelling remains unchanged.

    Similarly, the last syllable of စာတိုက် /sa-dai'/ "post office" is the
noun /tai'/ "masonry building"; after tone I /sa/ "writing, letter,"
the pronunciation changes from /tai'/ to /dai'/, but the writing remains constant.

    With few exceptions, ONE WRITTEN FORM OF A WORD IS USED regardless of
pronunciation changes in different spoken environments.

QUESTION 64:   Here are some examples of forms with unvoiced initial after
               tone IV and voiced initial after other tones. Write them out
               in transcription.

အိမ်ကို   _____   နောက်ကို   _____

            /qein-gou/   /nau'kou/

ကြက်သား:   _____   အမဲသား:   _____

            /ce'tha:/   /qame:dha:/

ခြောက်ဆယ်   _____   ငါးဆယ်   _____

            /hcau'hse/   /nga:ze/

ကို: ထောင် _____   ရှစ် ထောင် _____

    /kou:daun/   /hyi'htaun/

လို ချင် တယ် _____   လုပ် ချင် တယ် _____

    /lou-jin-de/   /lou'hcin-de/

QUESTION 65:   Now write the following words in transcription.

နှ င်: ခဲ _____   ကျယ် ကျယ် _____

    /hnin:ge:/   /ce-je/

ရာ သိ _____   က န် တော် ကြီး: _____

    /ya-dhi/   /kan-do-ji:/

မ နေ့ က _____   ဆေး: ဆေး: _____

    /manei.ga./   /hsei:zei:/

ရု ပ်ရှ င် ပွဲ _____   မီး: ဖို ချောင် _____

    /you'hyin-bwe:/   /mi:bou-jaun/

QUESTION 66:   Now try writing some sentences in transcription. These are
      quite basic, and you should recognize most of the words, so
      try to space correctly between them. The answers are in a
      separate key with translations.

1.   နေ ပါ စေ

_____

2.   မာ ရဲ့. လာ: ရှ င်

_____

3.   ဆေး: ရုံ ဒီ မှာ မ ရှိ ပါ ဘူး:

_____

4.   ဟို မှာ မီး: ရ ထာ: ဘူ တာ ရုံ

_____

5.   ထမင်းဆိုင်ဘယ်ဘက်မှာလဲ

_____

6.   ဘာမှမသောက်ပါဘူး

_____

7.   ခေါက်ဆွဲကြော်မစားချင်ဘူးလား

_____

8.   သူတို့အမေရိကန်လူမျိုးမဟုတ်ပါဘူး

_____

Key:

1.   /nei-ba-zei/

     "Never mind." "Let it go."

2.   /ma-ye.la: hyin/

     "How do you do, sir/madam?"

3.   /hsei:youn di-hma mahyi.ba-bu:/

     "The hospital isn't here."

4.   /hou-hma mi:yahta: bu-da-youn/

     "There's the railroad station."

5.   /htamin:zain be-be'hma-le:/

     "Which way is the restaurant?"

6.   /ba-hma. mathau'pa-bu:/

     "(I) won't have anything to drink."

7.   /hkau'hswe:jo masa:jin-bu:la:/

     "Don't you want some fried noodles?"

8.   /thu-dou. qamei-yi.kan lu-myou: mahou'pa-bu:/

     "They're not Americans."

CHAPTER 6

MISCELLANEOUS SYMBOLS

There are still a few more symbols for you to learn: the numerals, four special vowel symbols, four symbols used in literary style, and two punctuation marks.

The Numerals.

Here are the Burmese numerals with their names:

1	၁	/ti'/		6	၆	/hcau'/
2	၂	/hni'/		7	၇	/hkun-ni'/
3	၃	/thoun:/		8	၈	/hyi'/
4	၄	/lei:/		9	၉	/kou:/
5	၅	/nga:/		0	၀	/thoun-nya./

Each is written with a single stroke:

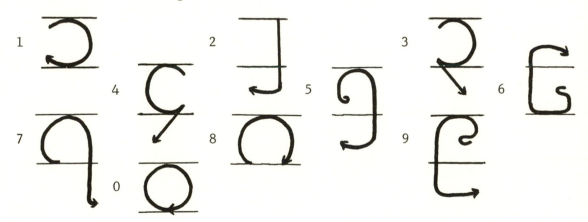

Practice writing them.

Some of these are identical with symbols used for letters:

ဂ /hyi'/ "eight" = ဂ /ga.nge/ "small ga"

84

ο /thoun-nya./ "zero" = ο /wa./

/ya.gau'/ "crooked <u>ya</u>" is sometimes distinguished from /hkun-ni'/ "seven" with a small internal loop:

ၵ /ya.gau'/ "crooked <u>ya</u>"

ၵ /hkun-ni'/ "seven"

However, one character frequently serves for both; they will not be distinquished in any of the exercises below.

The Burmese numerals combine in the same way as Arabic numerals. For example:

၁၂ /hse. hni'/ "12"

၁၃ο /taya. thoun:ze/ "130"

၆၉၅၄ /hcau'htaun kou:ya. nga:ze. lei:/ "6,954"

ဂ၅၄၉ၵ /hyi'thaun: nga:daun lei:ya. kou:ze. hkun-ni'/ "85,497"

QUESTION 67: For each numeral below give the value and name (e.g., 6 /hcau'/). If a symbol is also a consonant letter, give the syllable it represents in that value as well (e.g., ဂ /ga./). We have thrown in a few other consonant letters too, so be careful.

၃ _____   ၅ _____
3 /thoun:/   5 /nga:/

၉ _____   ဝ _____
9 /kou:/   /pa./

ο _____   ၂ _____
0 /thoun-nya./; /wa./   2 /hni'/

၄ _____   ၁ _____
/hta./   1 /ti'/

ဂ _____   ၇ _____
8 /hyi'/; /ga./   7 /hkun-ni'/; /ya./

c _____   G _____

           /nga./   6 /hcau'/

     ၄ _____

           4 /lei:/

QUESTION 68: Write the following numerals and consonants in Burmese.

/hni'/ _____   /nga:/ _____   /ti'/ _____

          J   ၅   ၁

/nga./ _____   /hkun-ni'/ _____   /ga./ _____

          c   ၇   ဂ

/lei:/ _____   /thoun:/ _____   /pa./ _____

          ၄   ၃   ပ

/thoun-nya./_____   /kou:/ _____   /hyi'/ _____

          o   ၉   ၈

/ya./ _____   /hcau'/ _____   /wa./ _____

       ရ (ဝ)   G   ၀

Special Vowel Symbols.

    Three new symbols and a combination of two you have already learned represent initial /q/ plus a vowel quality and a tone. These are:

        ဤ /qi./

        ဥ /qu./

        ဧ /qei:/ (sometimes /qei/)

        ဩ /qo:/

They are written:

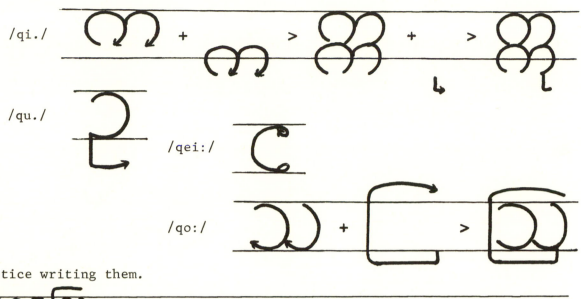

/qi./

/qu./   /qei:/

/qo:/

Practice writing them.

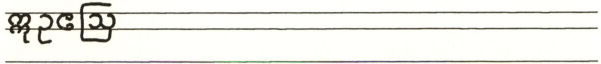

As you can see, ဩ /qo:/ is a combination of သ /tha./ and [◌ /ya. yi'/. It and ဥ /qu./ also combine with vowel and tone symbols to indicate other tones:

    ဉ /qu./   ဦ /qu/   ဦး /qu:/

    ဩ /qo:/   ေြာ် /qo/   ေြာ့ /qo./

ဤ and င do not combine with vowel or tone symbols in this way.

All of these syllables can also be written with အ /qa./ and the appro- priate vowel and tone symbols:

    အု /qu./   ေအာ /qo:/   အိ /qi./   ေအး /qei:/, etc.

QUESTION 69: Give the values of the following syllables.

င _____   အု _____   ဩ _____
   /qei:/ (/qei/)   /qu/   /qo:/

ဤ _____   ဦး: _____   ေအး: _____
   /qi./   /qu:/   /qei:/

င _____   သေဒ် _____   အော _____

        /nga./   /tho/   /qo:/

ဆု: _____   ရြည် _____   ၁ _____

        /hsu:/   /qo/   /qu./

QUESTION 70:   Give two Burmese writings for each of the following syllables.

/qu./ _____   /qo:/ _____

              ၁   အု   သ   အော

/qi./ _____   /qu/ _____

             အိ   အိ   ဥ   အု

/qo./ _____   /qei:/ _____

         ရြော့ အော့   င   အေ:

/qu:/ _____   /qo/ _____

         ဦး   အု:   ရြည် အေဒ်

Literary Symbols.

    Four other new symbols are used in literary style only:

        ဤ /qi/ "this"   (cf. colloquial ဒီ /di/)

        ၏ /qi./ final particle; "statement of fact"

                    (cf. colloquial တယ် /te/)

              noun particle; "possession"

                    (cf. colloquial ရဲ့ /ye./)

        ၌ /hnai'/ noun particle; "place where"

                    (cf. colloquial မှာ /hma/)

        ၍ /ywei./ subordinating particle; "prior circumstance"

                    (cf. colloquial use of the verb ပြီး: /pi:/)

These are written as follows:

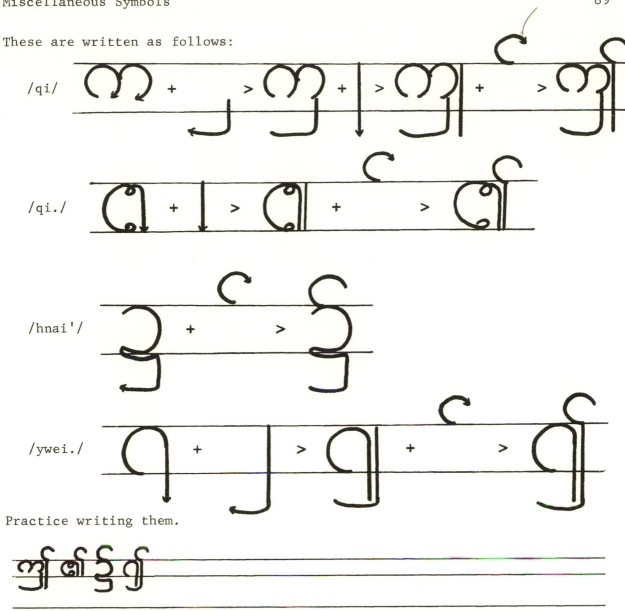

Practice writing them.

Of the last eight symbols, all but သ /qo:/ are designated with the term /qe'hkaya/ "letter of the alphabet" plus the value of the symbol:

ဉ /qe'hkaya qu./   ဧ /qe'hkaya qei:/

ဤ /qe'hkaya qi./   ဩ /qe'hkaya hnai'/

The symbol ဉ "is called /pa-li. qe'hkaya qi./ as it is used only in Pali words."[1]

---

1. Quoted from Robert B. Jones, Jr., and U Khin, <u>The Burmese Writing System</u> (American Council of Learned Societies, Washington, D.C., 1953).

QUESTION 71: Give the values of the following syllables.

ဦ _____   ဥ _____   ဣ _____
        /hnai'/   /qu./   /qi./

၂ _____   ၍ _____   ၊ _____
        /hni'/   /ywei./   /nga:/

ဩ _____   ၎ _____   ၕ _____
        /qo:/   /qi/   /qei:/ (/qei/)

၄ _____   ၏ _____   ဩော် _____
        /hta./   /qi./   /qo/

QUESTION 72: Give /qe'hkaya/ forms and numerals for the following syllables.

/qi/ _____   /qo:/ _____   /qu:/ _____
            ၍   ဩ   ဦ:

/hcau'/ _____   /qei:/ _____   /hnai'/ _____
            ၆   ၕ   ဦ

/thoun:/ _____   /lei:/ _____   /qi./ _____
            ၃   ၄   ဣ ၏

/kou:/ _____   /ti'/ _____   /ywei./ _____
            ၉   ၁   ၍

Punctuation.

Few punctuation marks are used in Burmese; the two traditional symbols are:

Symbol	Burmese Names	Translations
။	{ /pou'ma./ /pou'ci:/ }	section, paragraph

Symbol	Burmese Names	Translations
၊	{ /pou'thei:/	}
	{ /pou'ma.nge/	} little section

။ occurs at the end of any sentence, whether statement or question. The use of ၊ is similar to that of the comma in English. Here are some sample sentences with punctuation.

ဒါဘာလဲ ။

/da ba-le:/

"What's that?"

ကျွန်တော်ကတော့ ၊ မသွားဘူး ။

/cun-do-ga.do., mathwa:bu:/

"As for me, (I) won't go."

လက်နဲ့စားချင်သလား ၊ တူနဲ့စားချင်သလား ။

/le'ne. sa:jin-dhala:, tu-ne. sa:jin-dhala:/

"Do you want to eat with your fingers or with chopsticks?"

ဒီလိုဆိုရင် ၊ တရုပ်ထမင်းဆိုင်မှာဘဲစားရမယ် ။

/di-lou hsou-yin, tayou' htamin:zain-hma-be: sa:ya.me/

"If that's the case, we'll have to eat in the Chinese restaurant."

ဝက်သားဟင်းတခွက် ၊ ဟင်းသီးဟင်းရွက်ကြော်တခွက် ၊ ဟင်းချိုတခွက်နဲ့ထမင်း
ပေးပါအုန်း ။

/we'tha:hin: tahkwe', hin:dhi: hin:ywe'co tahkwe', hin:jou tahkwe'ne.
    htamin: pei:ba-qoun:/

"Give us a bowl of pork curry, a bowl of fried vegetables, a bowl of
    soup and some rice."

Besides these two punctuation marks, modern texts often use quotation marks or a raised comma to indicate direct speech.

CHAPTER 7

IRREGULARITIES

The great majority of Burmese words are written in the forms you have now
learned, but there are also other, less common, symbol combinations as well as
some unexpected values for familiar ones. Some of the more frequent of these
irregularities, which you are likely to encounter early in your reading, are
the subject of our final chapter. Your teachers will explain others as you
progress.

In some words, unpredictably, initial consonants represent sounds other
than those normally associated with them. A few examples are:[1]

> ထ /hta. hsin-du:/

>> ထား /da:/ "knife"   written: hta:

>> ထောင့် /daun./ "corner"   htaun.

> ဘ /ba.goun:/

>> ဘတ် /hpa'/ "to read"   ba'

>> မဟုတ်ဘူး /mahou'hpu:/ "isn't so"   mahou'bu:

> က /ka.ji:/

>> ကလေး /hkalei:/ "child"   kalei:

>> ကြီးတော် /ji:do/ "aunt"   ci:to

> ခ /hka.gwei:/

>> ခေါင်း /gaun:/ "head"   hkaun:

>> ကြာ: /ja:/ "between"   hca:

Certain of these, such as ဘ representing /hp/, are very common.

/r/ is not a part of the regular Burmese sound system. It occurs only in
loan words from other languages, where it is represented either by ရ /ya.gau'/

---

1. Many of the examples in this chapter are taken from Jones and Khin, <u>The
Burmese Writing System</u>.

or by ╟ /ya. yi'/, as in:

အေမရိကန် /qamei-ri.kan/ "American"

အာရပ် /qa-ra'/ "Arab"

ကရုဏာ /karu.na/ "pity, compassion"

သုံး /tri./ or /tari./ "three"

Irregular values for vowels are much less common. In some words ေ —
/thawei htou:/ represents /i/ instead of /ei/. For example:

အေစ့ /qasi./ "seed"

ေြမး /myi:/ "grandchild"

ေချး /hci:/ "lend; borrow"

Other irregular vowel pronunciations are still less common. Examples are:

ဘီး /bein:/ "wheel"   written: bi:

ဦး /qoun:/ "further, yet"   gu: (cf. p. 87)

These are written as open syllables but pronounced closed with final /-n/.
In each case the open syllable vowel quality shifts to the appropriate closed
syllable counterpart: /i/ to /ei/, /u/ to /ou/.

One of the most frequent types of irregularity involves syllables which
are written with vowel, tone, and/or final consonant symbols but are pronounced as atonic syllables. That is, all symbols other than the initial
consonant or consonant cluster are unpronounced. For example:

Vowel and tone symbols unpronounced:

ကူးတို့ /kadou./ "ferry"   written: ku:tou.

ငါးပိ /ngapi./ "fish paste"   nga:pi.

ပုဇွန် /pazun/ "shrimp"   pu.zun

ကုလားထိုင်/kalahtain/ "chair"   ku.la:htain

Final consonant symbols unpronounced:

ဘယ်သူ /badhu/ "who?"   written: be-thu

နှစ်ယောက်/hnayau'/ "two individuals"   hni'yau'

ကျွန်မ /cama./ "I" (woman speaking)   cun-ma.

နှုတ်ခမ်း: /hnahkan:/ "lip, edge"   written: <u>hnou'hkan:</u>

QUESTION 73: In each of the following words, the first syllable is atonic.
              Write them out in transcription.

အစ်မ _____   ကုလား: _____

/qama./   /kala:/

ပုလင်: _____   ငှက်ပျောသီး: _____

/palin:/   /hngapyo:dhi:/

ခက်ရင်: _____   စာရေး: _____

/hkayin:/   /sayei:/

နှာခေါင်: _____   သူငယ်ချင်: _____

/hnahkaun:/   /thange-jin:/

ကျား:သစ် _____   နှစ်လုံး: _____

/cathi'/   /hnaloun:/

On the other hand, such reduction is sometimes limited to medial symbols,
with the vowel and tone symbols pronounced. This, however, is much less frequent than the atonic reductions above. Examples are:

ကျာ   /ta/   "very red"   written: <u>tya</u>

ပြီး   /pi:/ "to finish"   <u>pyi:</u>

မိဘတွေ /mi.ba.dei/ "parents"   <u>mi.ba.twei</u>

Conversely, some syllables are pronounced with medial sounds not represented in the writing. For example:

ပစ်   /pyi'/ "to throw"   written: <u>pi'</u>

မင်   /hmin/ "ink"   <u>min</u>

သွား:နိုင်တယ် /thwa:hnain-de/ "can go"   <u>thwa:nain-te</u>

Besides these irregular values associated with regular initial consonant
and consonant cluster writings, there are some less common clusters with unexpected values. Some of these are unambiguous:

သျ /hy/ -   သျင် /hyin/ "lord"

                ဗသျူး /bahyu:/ "Malay"

in which only the medial /hy/ symbols are pronounced. But others represent
different readings in different words:

    ၀ -   ၀က် /hpwe'/, /hwe'/ "to hide"

             ၀ှုး:ဆို /houn: hsou/ "whoosh, whish"

             တောင်ဝှေး /taun-hmwei:/ "walking stick"

    လျှ -   လျှင် /hlin/, /hlyin/, /hlayin/ "if"

             လျှောက် /hyau'/ "to walk"

There are also irregular combinations of vowel and tone symbols. Some
forms that are usually tone I or tone II shift to tone III in certain contexts.
For example:

    /cun-do/ "I"   but: /cun-do./ "my"

    /hkin-bya:/ "you"   /hkin-bya./ "your"

    /thu/ "he"   /thu./ "his"

    /hse/ "ten"   /hse. thoun:/ "thirteen"

    /lou'pa-de/ "does"   /lou'pa.me/ "will do"

In some instances such shifts are marked with a regular tone III writing:

    ကျွန်တော် /cun-do/   to   ကျွန်တော့ /cun-do./

But frequently ◌့ /qau'ka. myi'/ is added to a tone I vowel symbol, even when
a separate tone III symbol is available, or to a syllable that already contains ◌း /hyei.ga. pau'/:

    ကျွန်တော် /cun-do/   to   ကျွန်တော့် /cun-do./

             for the expected   ကျွန်တော့

    သူ   /thu/   to   သူ့   /thu./

             for the expected   သု

    ဆယ် /hse/   to   ဆယ့်သုံး /hse. thoun:/

             for the expected   ဆဲ့ —

    လုပ်ပါတယ် /lou'pa-de/   to   လုပ်ပါ့မယ် /lou'pa.me/

             for the expected   — ◡ —

ခင်ဗျာ:   /hkin-bya:/   to   ခင်ဗျာ့   or   ခင်ဗျာ:   /hkin-b'ya./

for the expected   ခင်ဗျ

Many common irregularities involve closed syllables. You have learned
the "killed" consonants က် , စ် , တ် , ပ် , င် , န် , မ် , and the special
symbol ံ /thei:dhei: tin/ for writing closed syllables. However, although
they are less frequent, practically all the other consonant letters also occur
as finals. Most of these have predictable values like the regular symbols,
but some present special problems.

The most common irregular final is also the most ambiguous; ည် /nya. tha'/
"killed <u>nya</u>" has four values:

/i/   as in: ကြည့်.   /ci./ "look at"

/ei/ as in: ပြည်   /pyei/ "country"

/e/   as in: နာ:လည် /na: le/ "to understand

/in/ as in: စီစဉ် /si-zin/ "to arrange"

Of these, /i/ is the most frequent; many words written with ည် /nya. tha'/,
even though they are pronounced colloquially with /ei/ or /e/, also have an
alternate form with /i/, often as a reading pronunciation with a connotation
of more elevated or literary style. Thus the more literary pronunciation of
ပြည် is /pyi/, while /pyei/ is more colloquial; similarly, နာ:လည် is sometimes read /na: li/ as well as /na: le/. Since the value of ည် /nya. tha'/
is unpredictable, the pronunciation of each word in which it appears must be
memorized. In the last value /-in/, however, there is a tendency in modern
texts to use ဉ် /nya.galei: tha'/ "little killed <u>nya</u>" in place of ည် /nya.
tha'/. For example:

စီစဉ်   /si-zin/ "to arrange"

ကျဉ်:ၿမှာင်: /cin: myaun:/ "restricted, narrow"

Here there is no ambiguity; /-in/ is the regular value of ဉ် /nya.galei: tha'/.

Most other irregular finals have values that can be determined from the
consonant chart on page 29. This is true of all irregular finals (except ည်)
that appear in the first five horizontal rows. For these:

Consonants of the fifth vertical column represent /-n/

(that is, က် is like င် , န် , and မ် of the regular system)

Other consonants represent /'/ (tone IV)

When finals of these five rows occur with no vowel symbol, the vowel quality is determined by the final, as in the regular system. The quality associated with a particular consonant can again be determined from the consonant chart, that is:

Irregular finals of the	1st row	represent:	/e/	(like က်)
	2nd row		/i/	(like စ်)
	3rd-5th rows		/a/	(like တ်, ပ်)

Here are some words with these irregular finals:

မဂ်	/me'/	"passage, way"	ယဇ်	/yi'/	"sacrifice"
ဥပဒ်	/qu.ba'/	"danger"	ဘဏ်တိုက်	/ban-dai'/	"bank"

Of the remaining eight consonants at the bottom of the chart, you have already learned ယ် /ya. tha'/ as the regular writing for tone I /e/. Most of the others occur so rarely that we will omit them from this introduction, mentioning only the two most common ones: လ် /la. tha'/, which represents /-an/, and သ် /tha. tha'/, which represents /-a'/:

ဖလ်	/hpan/	"glass"	မာသ်ပဲ	/ma'pe:/	"bean"[2]

QUESTION 74: a) What are the values of ည် /nya. tha'/?

____

/i/, /ei/, /e/, /in/

How about ဉ် /nya.galei: tha'/?

____

/in/

b) Give the values you would expect for the following irregular finals.

–ဂ် ____________	–ဏ် ____________	–သ် ____________
/-e'/	/-an/	/-a'/
–ဗ် ____________	–ဇ် ____________	–လ် ____________
/-a'/	/-i'/	/-an/

2. The –ာ in the first syllable is discussed on the following page.

QUESTION 75:   Now write the following words in transcription.

အကျဉ်း:   _____   ယင်   _____

                    /qacin:/   /yi'/

ဥပဒ   _____   လေ့ကျင့်ခန်း:   _____

                    /qu.ba'/   /lei.jin.gan:/

အစဉ်   _____   မင်   _____

                    /qasin/   /me'/

ဘက်တိုက်   _____   စီစဉ်   _____

                    /ban-dai'/   /si-zin/

The vowel symbols $\overset{\circ}{-}$ and $\underset{L}{-}$ and the medial $\underset{\triangle}{-}$ /wa. hswe:/ usually have their regular closed syllable values when they occur with irregular finals:

သိသ   /thei'/   "monk's robe"   လိင်   /lein/   "sex, gender"

ပုဒ   /pou'/   "paragraph"   မုန်   /mou'/   "pagoda entrance"

အထွဋ်အမြတ်   /qahtu' qamya'/   "most excellent"

In other irregular closed syllables, the vowel symbols ၆— /thawei htou:/ and —ာ /yei: hca./ appear, usually with predictable values. In such syllables ၆— generally represents /i/ (compare the open syllables with ၆— on page 93):

ခေတ်   /hki'/   "era"

မဟာ ဝေသ ဝဏ္ဏ   /maha wi'tha. wun-na./[3]   (a title)

But —ာ is regularly unpronounced, the vowel quality of such syllables being determined by the final consonant, not the vowel symbol:

ဓါတ်   /da'/   "electricity"   လေယာဉ်ပျံ   /lei-yin-byan/   "airplane"

မာန်   /man/   "talk angrily"   ဖါယ်   /pe/   "exclude"

The combinations ၆—ာ and $\overset{\circ}{\underset{L}{-}}$ also appear with irregular finals, but their value is more difficult to predict. Besides its usual closed syllable value, ၆—ာ also appears occasionally with the value /u/:

----

3.   The form သ is discussed on page 101. Vertical consonant combinations
     are discussed beginning on the following page.

သောဋ္ဌိ သေန /thu'ti. thei-na./ (name of a prince)

ဖေါ့ဌ္ဌ   /hpu'ta'hpa./ "tangibility"

With irregular finals $\frac{o}{l}$ also sometimes has its regular closed syllable value, for example လှိုက်ဂူ /lain-gu/ "cave," but in other cases the final consonant is unpronounced, and $\frac{o}{l}$ has its open syllable value /ou/:

ကိုယ် /kou/ "body"   ဗိုလ် /bou/ "military officer"

မိုးယ်း /mou:/ "sky, rain"   ဂြိုဟ် /jou/ "planet"

QUESTION 76: Write out the following words in transcription. Here all syl-
             lables with final consonant have closed syllable values.

အာ ယွက် _____   လိင်   _____

              /qa-youn/   /lein/

ပါယ် _____   အ ထွဋ္ _____

              /pe/   /qahtu'/

ခေတ် _____   သိသ်   _____

              /hki'/   /thei'/

နာမ် _____   ဥ ပဒ်   _____

              /nan/   /qu.ba'/

ပုဒ် _____   လှိုက်ဂူ _____

              /pou'/   /lain-gu/

   In many words with a closed syllable preceding another syllable, the initial consonant of the second is written below the final consonant of the first.
For example, in the word ပုစ္ဆာ /pou'hsa/ "question," the initial ဆ of ဆာ
is written below the final ဒ် of ပုဒ် /pou'/. In such combinations $\stackrel{c}{}$ /qatha'/
is omitted -- the vertical writing already marks the upper consonant as final.
Any vowel or tone symbol written with such a vertical combination is associated
with the lower, or initial, consonant and forms a part of the second syllable.
Here are some examples:

   အနန္တ /qane'ga./ "immeasurable"   ကိစ္စ   /kei'sa./ "affair"

စက္ကူ။   /se'ku/ "paper"   သတ္တိ   /tha'ti./ "calamity"

ပုပ္ပါ:   /pou'pa:/ "(Mt.) Popa"   အက္ခရာ /qe'hkaya/ "letter of the
                                                                  alphabet"

Where the upper consonant represents /'/ tone IV, vertical combinations are unambiguous. But when the upper consonant represents final /-n/, there is no way to indicate the tone of the first syllable, since any tone symbol written with the combination is part of the second syllable. For example:

> စန္ဒာ:   /san-da:/ "fish trap"
>
> အိန္ဒိယ   /qein-di.ya./ "India"
>
> အိမ္မက်   /qein-me'/ "dream"
>
> သန္ဒေတဇ /than-dei taza./ "offspring of a plant"
>
> but: မန္ဒလေ:   /man:dalei:/ "Mandalay"
>
> ကြမ္မာ   /can:ma/ "healthy"

As you can see, there is no written indication that the မန် /man:/ of /man:dalei:/ is tonally different from the စန် /san-/ of /san-da:/. Note also that in such words as သန္ဒေတဇ /than-dei taza./, ေ — /thawei htou:/ intrudes into the middle of the preceding syllable.

QUESTION 77: Write the following words in transcription. For purposes of
practice here, all syllables with final /-n/ as upper member
of a vertical combination are tone I.

သမ္ဗန်   _____   ဒုက္ခ   _____
             /than-ban/   /dou'hka./

ပုန္နေ:မ _____   သိဒ္ဓိ   _____
             /poun-nei:ma./   /thei'di./

အာနန္ဒာ _____   လက်ခံဇု _____
             /qa-nan-da/   /le'hkan-zu./

ပုန္နာ:   _____   သတ္တိ   _____
             /poun-na:/   /tha'ti./

အဂ္ဂိရတ် _____   ဗန္ဓုလ _____

                    /qe'gi.ya'/   /ban-du.la./

ကိဿ _____   ကုမ္မာ _____

                    /kei'sa./   /koun-ma/

A number of other irregular writings for combinations of final and initial
consonants involve special forms of the letters. The most common is a minia-
ture form of င /nga. tha'/ written above the following initial consonant.
The resulting symbol ⚬ is given the special name /kin:zi:/. Examples of
its use are:

>   အင်္လန် /qin-galan/ "England"
>
>   အင်္ဂနေ့ /qin-ga-nei./ "Tuesday"
>
>   အင်္လိပ် /qin:galei'/ "English"
>
>   သင်္ဘော /thin:bo:/ "steamship"
>
>   ဂင်္ဂါ /gin.ga/ "Ganges"

Like final nasals in other vertical combinations, /kin:zi:/ is ambiguous as
to tone.

Other special forms for consonant combinations are less common. Some
examples are:

> ဉ /nya.galei:/ (final) plus စ /sa.loun:/ (initial) = ဉ္စ
>
> with စ reduced to fit inside the tail of ဉ :
>
> > ပဉ္စမ   /pyin-sama./ "fifth"
> >
> > ပဉ္စသီငါ:ပါ: /pyin-zathi nga:ba:/ "the five precepts"

> ဏ /na.ji:/ (final) plus ဍ /da. yin-gau'/ (initial) = ဏ္ဍ
>
> with ဍ turned on its side below ဏ :
>
> > မဏ္ဍပ်   /man:da'/ "pavilion"
> >
> > ဘဏ္ဍာရေး   /ban-da-yei:/ "finance"

> သ /tha./ (final) plus သ /tha./ (initial) = ဿ
>
> with the two consonants contracted into a single symbol called
> /tha.ji:/ "great tha":

ဖ သာ   /hpa'tha./   "perception"

ပိ သာ   /pei'tha/   "viss" (a unit of weight)

QUESTION 78: Write the following words in transcription. Once again, syl-
              lables with final /-n/ in vertical combination are tone I.

လ က်ာ   _____   ပြ သာ န်   _____
              /lin-ga/   /pya'tha'/

ကိ စ္စ   _____   ဒ ဏ္ဍာ ရိ   _____
              /kei'sa./   /dan-da-yi/

သ န်က်: စာ   _____   ပု ဏ္ဏာ :   _____
              /thin-gan:za/   /poun-na:/

အ နု သိ ဟ   _____   သိ ဒ္ဓိ   _____
              /qanou'thi-ha./   /thei'di./

လ က္ခ ရ   _____   သ ယ်ာ တော်   _____
              /le'hkan-zu./   /thin-ga-do/

In still another type of irregular final-initial combination, a consonant
or consonant cluster functions both as final of the first syllable and initial
of the second. Examples of single consonants in this use are:

ဒိ ဋ္ဌာ န်   /dei'htan/   "pray, supplicate"

မု ဆို :   /mou'hsou:/   "hunter"

ဘိ သိ က်   /bei'thei'/   "blessing" (cf. the use of /tha.ji:/
                                        သာ above)

ပ ညာ   /pyin-nya/   "knowledge"

In /dei'htan/ "pray," for example, ဋ္ဌ /hta. wun:be:/ represents both final /'/
for the first syllable ဒိ ဋ် /dei'/ -- so that ◌ိ has its closed syllable value
/ei/ -- and initial /ht/ for the following ဌာ န် /htan/.

Where a consonant cluster is involved, there is further ambiguity. In
some words both initial consonant symbol and medial symbol act as initial of
the second syllable:

ေယာ က်ျာ း   /yau'ca:/ "man"

ေသာ ြကာ ေန့   /thau'ca-nei./ "Friday"

But in others the consonant symbol acts only as final of the first syllable,
with the medial as initial of the second:

လ က်ျာ   /le'ya/ "right hand"

In some of these words ◌် /qatha'/ is present, in others not. Compare also
ြကိယာ /kari.ya/ "action; verb," in which medial [◌ျ /ya. yi'/ is separated
from initial က /ka.ji:/ and acts independently as initial of the second
syllable.

   A few final points will close our introduction of irregularities.

   Some of the /qe'hkaya/ symbols (page 89) combine with final consonants
to form closed syllables. When ◌ွိ /qi./ and ◌ု /qu./ occur in such syllables,
the vowel qualities shift to /ei/ and /ou/, just as those of ◌ိ /i./ and ◌ု
/u./ do. For example:

ꧠ ရ ြန့ သ ည်   /qein-dayei hse/ "reserved, restrained"

ၥ ꧠ န်   /qou'kahta./ "president"

On the other hand, ေ◌ /qei:/ in combination with final consonants loses its
vowel quality and represents only initial /q/:

ေ ည့် သ ည်   /qe.dhe/ "guest"

   In connection with ၃ /qe'hkaya qu./, there is another minor problem.
Near the beginning of this chapter we introduced the symbol ၃ /nya.galei:
tha'/. Without /qatha'/, ၃ /nya.galei:/ is the left half of ည /nya./, but
it is also the same as ၃ /qu./. Of course, when ၃ occurs as a final with
◌် there is no ambiguity, but /nya.galei:/ also occurs initially, as in:

၃ာ ဏ်   /nyan/ "intellect, reason"

This is, however, very rare. In general:

     ၃   as syllable initial represents /qu./

           as a final (with ◌်) represents /-in/

   In some words borrowed from foreign languages a syllable-final consonant
sound which does not normally occur in Burmese is represented by a "killed"
consonant in parentheses. For example:

ဘတ်(စ်)ကား : /baska:/, /ba'saka:/ "bus"

ဂျုံး(စ်) /jouns:/ "Jones"

ဒေါ့(ဂျ်) /doj./ "Dodge" (brand name)

One unique combination involves the numeral ၄ /lei:/ "four" plus ၌ /nga. tha'/ and —: /hyei.ga. pau'/. Together these form the literary expression:

၄၌: /lagaun:/ "the aforementioned"

The colloquial equivalent is အဲဒါ /qe:da/.

Now let us go back over the irregularities once more.

QUESTION 79: a) The values of the following forms are ambiguous. Give as many readings for each as you can.

ပြည် _____

/pyi/, /pyei/, /pye/, /pyin/

ကုမ္မာ _____

/koun-ma/, /koun:ma/, /koun.ma/

လက်ျာ _____

/le'ya/, /le'ca/

ဂင်္ဂါ _____

/gin-ga/, /gin:ga/, /gin.ga/

b) In the following words, all syllables but the last are atonic. Write them out in transcription.

ခက်ရင်: _____   စာရေး: _____

/hkayin:/   /sayei:/

သဒ္ဒါ _____   နှစ်လုံး: _____

/thada/   /hnaloun:/

ပုလင်း: _____   ကုလားထိုင် _____

/palin:/   /kalahtain/

QUESTION 80: Give the values of the following expressions.

Burmese	Value	Burmese	Value
မုန်	/mou'/	သူ့	/thu./
လက္ခဏဒ	/le'hkan-zu./	ကုတ္တီရတ်	/qei'hti.ya'/
လိင်	/lein/	ဒုက္ခ	/dou'hka./
ပါယ်	/pe/	လေ့ကျင့်ခက်း	/lei.jin.gan:/
ဥစ္စာ	/qou'sa/	ဥပုသ်	/qu.bou'/
ခေတ်	/hki'/	ယဉ်	/yi'/
သွားပါမယ်	/thwa:ba.me/	ကုသ	/qei'tha./
ပုပ္ပါး	/pou'pa:/	ကျဉ်းမြောင်း	/cin: myaun:/
ဆယ့်လေး	/hse. lei:/	သိဒ္ဓိ	/thei'di./
မဂ်	/me'/	လေယာဉ်ပုံ	/lei-yin-byan/

For many words, an irregular writing such as those described in this
chapter is standard; for others, however, there is a regular spelling as well
as the irregular one. And even within the regular system there is some variation in the writing of words whose sounds can be represented in more than
one way. Here a few examples of such alternative spellings:

ရင်   /yin/   "if"   also written: ဝင်

ကြော်   /co/   "fry"   ကျော်

ဆံ   /hsan/ "husked rice"   ဆန်

ထား:   /da:/   "knife"   ဒါ:   or   ဓါ:

ဘတ်   /hpa'/ "to read"   ဖတ်

ချေ:   /hci:/ "to lend; borrow"   ချီ:

ဦး:   /qoun:/ "further, yet"   အုန်: or   အုံ:

ကျွမာ   /can:ma/ "healthy'   ကျွမာ or   ကျန်:မာ

ပြီ:   /pi:/   "to finish"   ပိ:

မင်   /hmin/ "ink"   မှင်

ရှင်   /hyin/ "lord"   ရှင်

ကြိယာ   /kari.ya/ "action, verb"   ကရိယာ

In modern texts there is some tendency to standardize the spelling, but many
variations still occur. Be alert for such alternative writings as you go on
to read Burmese texts.

     Now go to the Summary Test in Appendix A, which will take you through a
complete review of the Burmese writing system.

SUMMARY TEST

SECTION A: Write the following expressions in Burmese. In this section use
            only regular writings; we'll take up the irregularities in the
            following sections.

1. /hnge'/ _____ 2. /hta./ _____

3. /caun./ _____ 4. /lwe/ _____

5. /do/ _____ 6. /thi'thi:/ _____

7. /hnan./ _____ 8. /byou./ _____

9. /qu:/ _____ 10. /nyun./ _____

11. /hsaun: qahka/ _____ 12. /hpwin./ _____

13. /hcou'/ _____ 14. /qo/ _____

15. /zi./ _____ 16. /le'hsaun/ _____

17. /pei'/ _____ 18. /hsai'ka:/ _____

19. /qi-dhou./ _____ 20. /qain/ _____

21. /po.lei/ _____ 22. /hlein/ _____

23. /we'tha:/ _____ 24. /ce'qu./ _____

25. /tahka talei/ _____   26. /houn:/ _____

27. /yu./ _____   28. /hkau'hswe:/_____

29. /hyu'/ _____   30. /qatwe'/ _____

31. /go:/ _____   32. /hmwei/ _____

33. /tahkau'/ _____   34. /qaya.dha/ _____

SECTION B: Write the following expressions in transcription. Here you should
            be prepared to see some irregular forms.

1. ဂဠုန် _____   2. မျှော်စင် _____

3. လူမျိုး _____   4. ၄၁န _____

5. မုတ်ဆိတ် _____   6. နဂါး _____

7. သိဒ္ဓ _____   8. လုံလောက် _____

9. ရှိပါစေ _____   10. နှင်းခဲ _____

11. ခေတ် _____   12. ပိုက်ဆံ _____

13. ကျောင်းသူ _____   14. ဘီယာ _____

15. လေယာဉ်ပုံ _____   16. အောက်ထပ် _____

17. ကောက်ညှင်း _____   18. သစ်သီး _____
    ပေါင်း

19. ဒါပေတဲ့ _____   20. ပါယ် _____

21. ခက _____   22. ငါးဆယ် _____

23. ၈၈ _____   24. မုန့်ဟင်းခါး _____

25. ဝက်ဝံ _____   26. ၄င်း _____

27. စာအုပ် _____   28. သွား၍ _____

29. မိတ်ဆွေ _____   30. ဟင်းချို _____

31. ပူဇော် _____   32. ညဂုတ်လ _____

33. ၃၀ _____   34. အစိမ်း _____

35. ပြေးပြေး _____   36. ၃၈၁ _____

37. ကျွန်တော် _____   38. ချက်လက်မှတ် _____

39. ဆို၏ _____   40. ၆၀ _____

41. ရေနွေး _____   42. အပေါ်ထပ် _____

43. စီစဉ် _____   44. တယောက်စာ _____

45. ရုပိကာ _____   46. ရန်ကုန်၍ _____

47. လွှတ် _____   48. ပဌမ _____

49. ကုသ _____   50. သံရုံး _____

51. ရို:ရိမ် _____   52. ပြောင်းရွှေ့ _____

53. ယဇ် _____   54. ဂဏန်း _____

55. ၄၀ _____   56. တောရွာ _____

57. သိမ်ကြီးဈေး _____   58. ဒုက္ခ _____

59. အဝတ် _____ 60. စရိဒ္ဓ _____

SECTION C: Transcribe the following sentences. They are quite basic, and you
            should recognize most of the vocabulary, so try to space properly
            between words -- and remember that the initial consonant voicing
            changes (page 80) occur only <u>within</u> words.

1.   နေ ကောင်းရဲ့လား ဦးဝေလင်း

      _____

2.   ရုပ်ရှင်ပွဲ ဘယ်တော့ ပြမလဲ ။

      _____

3.   ထော ပတ်လို ချင်ပါတယ် ။

      _____

4.   သူ့ နံ မယ် ဘယ်လို ခေါ်သလဲ ။

      _____

5.   မနေ့ ကဟို သူ ရန် ကုန်မြို့ က လာ တယ် ။

      _____

6.   ကျေးဇူးတင်ပါတယ် ။   ကိစ္စ မရှိ ပါ ဘူး ။

      _____

7.   ကိုလှ မောင် ဘယ်ကို သွားမလဲ ။

      _____

8.   မီးရထား ဆ ယ့် နှစ် နာရီ ထွက်မယ် ။

      _____

9.   ဒီဟာ ခဲဘံ လား၊ က လောင်တံ လား ။

      _____

၁၀.   ကြက်ဥ ကြော်မ စား ချင်ဘူး လား ။

_____

၁၁.   ဟို ကျောင်းဆရာမ ဘယ်မြို့သူလဲ ။

_____

၁၂.   ဒါကို ဗမာ လို ဆေး ရုံ့ လို့, ခေါ် ပါတယ် ။

_____

၁၃.   ရုပ်ရှင် ရုံညာ ဘက်မှာလား ၊ ဘယ်ဘက်မှာ လား ။

_____

၁၄.   ဦး လှ မောင် တ ရုပ် ကျောင်းဆရာ မဟုတ်ဘူး ။

_____

၁၅.   နက်ဖြင်ခါ မော်လမြိုင်မြို့ကိုသွားပုံမယ် ။

_____

SUMMARY TEST: ANSWERS.

SECTION A:

1. ငှက်   2. ထ

3. ကျောင့်၊ ကြောင့်   4. လှယ်

5. ဒေါ်၊ မော်   6. သစ်သီး

7. နှန့်၊ နှဲ့၊ (နှဲ့)   8. မျိုု၊ ဗြိုု၊ ဘျိုု၊ ကြိုု

9. ဦး၊ အှူး   10. ညွန့်၊ ညွဲ့၊ (ညွဲ့)

11. ဆောင်းအခါ   12. ဖှင့်

13. ချက်၊ ချပ်၊ ခြက်၊ ခြပ်   14. ညြော်၊ အော်

15. ဇီ၊ ရှိ   16. လက်ဆောင်

17. ဝိတ်၊ ဝိပ်   18. ဆိုက်ကား

19. ဤသို့၊ အီသို့   20. အိုင်

21. ပေါ့လေ   22. လွှန်၊ လွှမ်

23. ဝက်သား   24. ကျက်ဥ၊ ကြက်ဥ၊ ကျက်အှူ၊ ကြက်အှူ

25. တခါတလေ   26. ဟှုန်း၊ ဟုံး

27. ယှူ၊ ရှူ   28. ခေါက်ဆွဲ

29. ယွှတ်၊ ယွှပ်၊ ရွှတ်၊ ရွှပ်   30. အတွက်

31. ဂေါ   32. မွှ

33. တခေါက်   34. အယသာ၊ အရသာ

SECTION B:

1. /galoun/   2. /hmyo-zin/

3. /lu-myou:/   4. /hta-na./

5. /mou'hsei'/   6. /naga:/

7. /thei'di./   8. /loun-lau'/

9. /hyi.ba-zei/   10. /hnin:ge:/

11. /hki'/   12. /pai'hsan/

13. /caun:dhu/   14. /bi-ya/

15. /lei-yin-byan/   16. /qau'hta'/

17. /kau'hnyin:baun:/   18. /thi'thi:/

19. /da-bei-de./   20. /pe/

21. /hkana./   22. /nga:ze/

23. /qei:qei:/   24. /moun.hin:ga:/

25. /we'wun/   26. /lagaun:/

27. /sa-qou'/   28. /thwa:ywei./

29. /mei'hswei/   30. /hin:jou/

31. /pu-zo/   32. /qo:gou'la./

33. /thoun:ze/   34. /qasein:/

35. /hpyei:byei:/   36. /qou'sa/

37. /cun-do/   38. /hce'le'hma'/

39. /hsou-qi./   40. /hcau'hse/

41. /yei-nwei:/   42. /qapo-da'/

43. /si-zin/   44. /tayau'sa/

45. /du.bi.ga/   46. /yan-goun-hnai'/

47. /hlu'/   48. /pahtama./

49. /qei'tha./   50. /than-youn:/

51. /sou:yein/   52. /pyaun:hywei./

53. /yi'/   54. /ganan:/

55. /lei:ze/   56. /to:ywa/

57. /thein-ji:zei:/   58. /dou'hka./

59. /qawu'/   60. /sayan-ngwei/

SECTION C:

1. /nei kaun:ye.la:, qu: wei lin:/
    "Are you well, U Wei Lin?"

2. /you'hyin-bwe: be-do. pya.male:/
   "When will the movie be shown?"

3. /hto:ba' lou-jin-ba-de/
   "I want some butter."

4. /thu. nan-me be-lou hko-dhale:/
   "What is his name?"

5. /manei.ga. hou lu yan-goun myou.ga. la-de/
   "That man came from Rangoon yesterday."

6. /cei:zu: tin-ba-de/   /kei'sa. mahyi.ba-bu:/
   "Thank you."   "Don't mention it."

7. /kou hla. maun be-gou thwa:male:/
   "Where are you going, Ko Hla Maung?"

8. /mi:yahta: hse. hnana-yi htwe'me/
   "The train will leave at twelve o'clock."

9. /di ha hke:dan-la:, kalaun-dan-la:/
   "Is this a pencil or a pen?"

10. /ce'qu.jo masa:jin-bu:la:/
    "Don't you want some fried eggs?"

11. /hou caun: hsaya-ma. be-myou.dhu-le:/
    "What city is that woman teacher a native of?"

12. /da-gou bama-lou hsei:youn-lou. hko-ba-de/
    "In Burmese that's called a 'hospital.'"

13. /you'hyin-youn nya-be'hma-la:, be-be'hma-la:/
    "Is the movie theater to the right or to the left?"

14. /qu: hla. maun tayou' caun: hsaya mahou'hpu:/
    "U Hla Maung is not a Chinese teacher."

15. /ne'hpyin-ga mo-lamyain myou.gou thwa:ba.me/
    "Tomorrow (I) will go to Moulmein."

APPENDIX B

SPELLING

Words are spelled in Burmese with the names of the symbols which we have introduced throughout the book. While these names are often rather long and complicated, once you have mastered them the actual process of spelling is, for the most part, quite simple. With few exceptions, the symbols which make up a word are spelled in the same order in which they are written. Here are some examples:

က   /ka./ "to dance"
      spelled: /ka.ji:/

ထု   /htu./ "to carve, engrave"
      spelled: /hta. hsin-du:, tahcaun: ngin/

ရဲ   /ye:/ "bold"
      spelled: /ya.gau', nau' pyi'/

မီး   /mi:/ "fire"
      spelled: /ma., loun:ji: tin hsan hka', hyei.ga. pau'/

ပေါ   /po/ "clear"
      spelled: /thawei htou:, pa.zau', yei: hca., hyei. htou:/

သင့်   /thin./ "convenient"
      spelled: /tha., nga. tha', qau'ka. myi'/

လိုက် /lai'/ "to follow"
      spelled: /la., loun:ji: tin, tahcaun: ngin, ka. tha'/

With the medial symbols, however, the spelling and writing orders differ. You learned the writing order (on page 43):

◌ၟ /wa. hswe:/ before   ◌ှ /ha. htou:/ before   { ◌ျ /ya. pin./
                                                      or
                                                     ◌ြ /ya. yi'/ }

The spelling order is:

◌ှ /ha. htou:/ before { ◌ျ /ya. pin./
                           or
                          ◌ြ /ya. yi'/ } before   ◌ၟ /wa. hswe:/

115

Compare, for example, the writing and spelling orders of the following words:

ေကြ   /cwei/ "to drop off"

    written: ေ + က + ◌ၟ + ◌ြ

    spelled: /thawei htou:, ka.ji:, ya. pin., wa. hswe:/

ခြွ   /hcwa./ "cause to swell"

    written: ခ + ◌ၟ + ◌ြ

    spelled: /hka.gwei:, ya. yi', wa. hswe:/

ှွာ   /hnwa/ "to skin"

    written: န + ◌ၟ + ◌ျ + ◌ာ

    spelled: /na.(nge), ha. htou:, wa. hswe:, yei: hca./

မြှု   /hmyu/ "to delight, allure"

    written: မ + ◌ျ + ◌ြ + ◌ု

    spelled: /ma., ha. htou:, ya. yi', hnahcaun: ngin/

Only a few other forms require special mention.

Most of the /qe'hkaya/ symbols (page 89) do not combine with other symbols within a syllable and are simply spelled with their names. When ဥ /qe'hkaya qu./ combines with vowel and tone symbols, the syllable is spelled as if ဥ were an initial consonant; for example:

ဦး   /qu:/ "uncle"

    spelled: /qe'hkaya qu., loun:ji: tin hsan hka', hyei.ga. pau'/

On the other hand, the elements of သြ /qo:/ are spelled out in the normal order, i.e.:

ေသြာ် /qo/ "Oh!"

    spelled: /thawei htou:, tha., ya. yi', yei: hca., hyei. htou'/

Of the irregular forms in Chapter 7, certain closed syllable writings are spelled with special expressions.

Vertical writings are spelled in two ways. If one symbol occurs as both upper and lower member of a vertical combination, the expression /hnaloun: hsin./ "two characters stacked" follows the name of the consonant, as in:

ၐႃ႙ /se'ku/ "paper"

       spelled: /sa.loun:, ka.ji: hnaloun: hsin., hnahcaun: ngin/

          that is: "two great <u>ka</u>'s stacked"

အိမ္မက် /qein-me'/ "to dream"

       spelled: /qa., loun:ji: tin, ma. hnaloun: hsin., ka. tha'/

          that is: "two <u>ma</u>'s stacked"

But if the two members are different symbols, the expression /-qau'ka./
"below" follows the first; for example:

ဒုက္ခ /dou'hka./ "trouble, pain"

       spelled: /da.dwei:, tahcaun: ngin, ka.ji:qau'ka. hka.gwei:/

          that is: "below great <u>ka</u>, curved <u>hka</u>"

သန္တတ /than-dei taza./ "offspring of a plant"

       spelled: /tha., thawei htou:, na.nge-qau'ka. da. qau'hcai',
              ta. wun:bu, za.gwe:/

          that is: "below small <u>na</u>, bottom-indented <u>da</u>"

The second rule also applies to such specialized forms as ဉ္ဉ and ဏ္ဍ ,
which are, respectively, /nya.galei:qau'ka. sa.loun:/ "below little <u>nya</u>,
round <u>sa</u>," and /na.ji:qau'ka. da. yin-gau'/ "below great <u>na</u>, crooked-breasted
<u>da</u>."

The rare combination ဍ္ဎ is spelled with the expression /-hte:ga./
"inside" to describe the position of the second consonant, that is: /da.
yei-hmou'hte:ga. da. yin-gau'/ "inside water-dipper <u>da</u>, crooked-breasted <u>da</u>."

On the other hand, ◌ᜳ /kin:zi:/ is treated like the vowel symbols and
spelled after the consonant over which it is written, as in:

အင်္ဂလန် /qin-galan/ "England"

       spelled: /qa., ga.nge, kin:zi:, la., na. tha'/

သင်္ဘော /thin:bo:/ "steamship"

       spelled: /tha., thawei htou:, ba.goun:, kin:zi:, yei: hca./

ဿ /tha.ji:/ "great <u>tha</u>" is treated like a simple consonant:

ပိဿာ /pei'tha/ "viss"

       spelled: /pa.zau', loun:ji: tin, tha.ji:, yei: hca./

In combinations such as ကျ , /qatha'/ is spelled following the initial consonant symbol:

ယောက်ျား /yau'ca:/ "man"

   spelled: /thawei htou:, ya. pale', yei: hca., ka. tha', ya.
         pin., yei: hca., hyei.ga. pau'/

လက်ျာ /le'ya/ "right hand"

   spelled: /la., ka. tha', ya. pin., yei: hca./

In those foreign words which include finals in parentheses, the enclosed symbol is followed by the expression /kwin: hka'/ "surrounded in parentheses":

ဘတ်(စ်)ကား:/baska:/ "bus"

   spelled: /ba.goun:, ta. tha', sa. tha' kwin: hka', ka.ji:,
         yei: hca., hyei.ga. pau'/

  that is: "killed <u>sa</u> in parentheses"

APPENDIX C

THE SYMBOLS OF BURMESE

There follows a complete list of the symbols which occur in the Burmese writing system, with the names transcribed, translated, and written out in Burmese. In so far as possible, symbols within one category have been listed in alphabetical order, but that order is not standardized in Burmese reference works, so you should be prepared for some variation. Certain specialized combinations of symbols (e.g. ေ — ာ , ို) are also included in brackets to show their alphabetical order.

Initial consonant symbols:

က	/ka.ji:/	great ka	ကကြီး
ခ	/hka.gwei:/	curved hka	ခခွေး
ဂ	/ga.nge/	small ga	ဂငယ်
ဃ	/ga.ji:/	great ga	ဃကြီး
င	/nga./		
စ	/sa.loun:/	round sa	စလုံး
ဆ	/hsa.lein/	twisted hsa	ဆလိမ်
ဇ	/za.gwe:/	split za	ဇကွဲ
ဈ	*/za. myin-zwe:/	bridle za	ဈမြင်းဆွဲ
ည	/nya./		
[ဉ	/nya.galei:/	little nya	ဉကလေး]
ဋ	*/ta. talin:jei'/	bier-hook ta	ဋသံလျင်းချိတ်
ဌ	/hta. wun:be:/	duck hta	ဌဝမ်းဘဲ
ဍ	/da. yin-gau'/	crooked-breasted da	ဍရင်ကောက်

* Starred forms are pronounced irregularly; compare the Burmese writings.

ဎ	/da. yei-hmou'/	water-dipper da	ဎရေမှုတ်
ဏ	/na.ji:/	great na	ဏကြီး
တ	/ta. wun:bu/	pot-bellied ta	တဝမ်းပူ
ထ	/hta. hsin-du:/	elephant-fetter hta	ထဆင်ထူး
ဒ	/da.dwei:/	twisted da	ဒထွေး
ဓ	/da. qau'hcai'/	bottom-indented da	ဓအောက်ခြိုက်
န	/na.nge/ (or /na./)	small na	နငယ်
ပ	/pa.zau'/	steep (sided) pa	ပစောက်
ဖ	*/hpa. qou'htou'/	capped hpa	ဖဦးထုပ်
ဗ	*/ba. lahcai'/	top-indented ba	ဗထက်ခြိုက်
ဘ	/ba.goun:/	hump-backed ba	ဘကုန်း
မ	/ma./		
ယ	*/ya. pale'/	supine ya	ယပက်လက်
ရ	/ya.gau'/	crooked ya	ရကောက်
လ	/la./		
ဝ	/wa./		
သ	/tha./		
ဟ	/ha./		
ဠ	/la.ji:/	great la	ဠကြီး
အ	/qa./		

Medial symbols (consonant cluster symbols):

ျ	/ya. pin./	supporting ya	ယပင့်
ြ	/ya. yi'/	encircling ya	ရရစ်
ွ	/wa. hswe:/	suspended wa	ဝဆွဲ
ှ	/ha. htou:/	thrust-in ha	ဟထိုး

The Symbols of Burmese

Vowel symbols:

ー ာ (ーါ)	/yei: hca./	(line) drawn down	ရေးချ
◌ုံ	/loun:ji: tin/	big circle put on	လုံးကြီးတင်
◌ုံ	/loun:ji: tin hsan hka'/	big circle put on, with a grain of rice added	လုံးကြီးတင်ဆန်ခတ်
◌ု (ーျ)	/tahcaun: ngin/	one stroke drawn out	တချောင်းငင်
◌ူ (ーႂ) */hnahcaun: ngin/	two strokes drawn out	နှစ်ချောင်းငင်
ေ ー	/thawei htou:/	thrust in front	သဝေထိုး
◌ဲ	*/nau' pyi'/	thrown backwards	နောက်ပစ်

[ေ ー ာ (ေ ーါ) /thawei htou:, yei: hca./]

[◌ေု (◌ေု)   /loun:ji: tin, tahcaun: ngin/]

Tone symbols:

◌့	/qau'ka. myi'/	stopped below	အောက်ကမြစ်
◌း	/hyei.ga. pau'/	dots ahead	ရှေ့ကပေါက်
◌ို	/hyei. htou:/	thrust forward	ရှေ့ထိုး

Special symbols for, or involved with, final consonants:

◌်	/qatha'/	killer	အသတ်
◌ိ	/thei:dhei: tin/	little thing put on	သေးသေးတင်
◌ င်	/kin:zi:/	(the name of this symbol)	ကင်းစီး
သ	/tha.ji:/	great tha	သကြီး

The /qe'hkaya/ symbols:

ဣ	/pa-li. qe'hkaya qi./	Pali alphabet symbol qi.	ပါဠိအက္ခရာဣ
ဤ	/qe'hkaya qi/	alphabet symbol qi (literary: "this")	အက္ခရာဤ
ဥ	/qe'hkaya qu./	alphabet symbol qu.	အက္ခရာဥ

၆	/qeʼhkaya qei:/	alphabet symbol <u>qei:</u>	အက္ခရာ ၆
[သ	/tha., ya. yiʼ/]		
၌	/qeʼhkaya hnaiʼ/	alphabet symbol <u>hnaiʼ</u> (literary: "at, in")	အက္ခရာ ၌
၍	/qeʼhkaya ywei./	alphabet symbol <u>ywei.</u> (literary: "having [done]")	အက္ခရာ ၍
၏	/qeʼhkaya qi./	alphabet symbol <u>qi.</u> (literary final particle or possession)	အက္ခရာ ၏

The numerals:

၁	/tiʼ/	one	တစ်
၂	/hniʼ/	two	နှစ်
၃	/thoun:/	three	သုံး
၄	/lei:/	four	လေး
၅	/nga:/	five	ငါး
၆	/hcauʼ/	six	ခြောက်
၇	*/hkun-niʼ/	seven	ခုနှစ်
၈	/hyiʼ/	eight	ရှစ်
၉	/kou:/	nine	ကိုး
၀	*/thoun-nya./	zero	သုည

Punctuation:

။	{ /pouʼma./ { /pouʼci:/	section, paragraph	{ ပုဒ်မ { ပုဒ်ကြီး:
၊	{ /pouʼthei:/ { /pouʼma.nge/	little section	{ ပုဒ်သေး: { ပုဒ်မငယ်